PARENTING YOUR CHILD WITH AUTISM

PRACTICAL STRATEGIES TO MEET THE CHALLENGES AND HELP YOUR FAMILY THRIVE

LUCY TALBOTT

PARENTHOOD PRESS

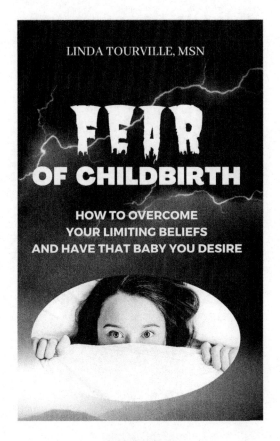

the
PREGNANCY
HANDBOOK
for
FIRST-TIME
MOMS

A Comprehensive Guide
Covering Weekly
Fetal Development,
Maternal Changes,
Prenatal Tests,
and Making
Informed Decisions

LINDA TOURVILLE, MSN

For the seven brightest lights in my life

Breonna

Ella

Brenden

Jace

Lucas

Greta

Noah

CONTENTS

Introduction   xi

1. AFTER THE DIAGNOSIS – WHAT NOW?   1
   Mary and Jack   2
   This is the Same Child You Have Always Loved   4
   Children With Autism Are Achieving Great Things   5
   Positive Coping Strategies   6
   Acknowledging the Diagnosis   9
   You Can Only Change Yourself   10
   Sharing the News   11
   What Should You Tell Your Child?   12
   Chapter Summary   13

2. STRAIGHT TALK ABOUT AUTISM   15
   What is Autism Spectrum Disorder?   15
   Myths Surrounding Autism   16
   Are Autistic Brains Different?   18
   Signs of Autism   18
   Are There Different Types of Autism?   19
   Autism: Causes and Risk Factors   20
   Common Interventions for Autism   20
   Understanding the Autism Spectrum   22
   Autism Vocabulary   24
   The Challenges of Raising a Child With Autism   25
   Penny and Kara   26
   Chapter Summary   27

3. PRIORITIZE YOUR CHILD'S SAFETY AND EDUCATION   29
   Home Design and Safety   29
   Prepare Financially for Autism   32
   Early Intervention and Therapies   34
   Being Your Child's Advocate is a Lifetime Journey   39
   Chapter Summary   41

4. LIVING WITH AUTISM   43
   Keep Records and Organize Your Files   43
   Support Your Other Children   44
   Create a Structured Home Environment   45

Understand Your Child's Behavior 47

Deal With Your Child's Behavior 49

Interact With Your Child 52

Support Your Child's Growth 53

Identify and Deal With Common Struggles 54

Receive Parental Training in Behavior Management 55

Chapter Summary 55

5. YOU DON'T HAVE TO DO THIS ALONE 57

Start From Ground-Up: Build Healthy Family Dynamics 57

Build a Strong Relationship With Your Partner 59

Parenting an Autistic Child is Stressful 59

Take Conflict Seriously 61

Rely on Your Extended Family 61

Acknowledge Your Child's Contributions to The Family 62

Build a Supportive Team 63

Key Sources of Support 65

Chapter Summary 68

6. PREPARE FOR YOUR CHILD'S FUTURE FINANCIAL
INDEPENDENCE 71

Financial Planning for Two Generations 71

Plan for Your Child's Living Arrangements 72

Autism and Employment 74

Questions to Ask Yourself 75

Find a Guardian 76

Estate and Financial Planning for Your Child 78

Empower Your Child to Live More Independently 81

Chapter Summary 83

7. MISTAKES TO AVOID 85

Hiding Your Child's Diagnosis 85

Assuming Challenging Behavior is a Tantrum 86

Thinking Your Child Isn't Smart 87

Thinking Autism is the Same Thing as Social Aversion 88

Expecting Others to Be Knowledgeable About Autism 88

Comparing Your Child to Others 89

Forcing Interests Onto Your Child 90

Refusing to Ask For Help 91

Drawing Unwarranted Conclusions 91

Overindulging Your Child or Being Excessively Vigilant 92

Putting Yourself Last on the List 93

Chapter Summary 94

8. CARE FOR THE CAREGIVER 95
   Harness the Power of Self-Care Routines 95
   Prioritize Self-Kindness Over Self-Confidence 97
   Remember the Power of Your Thoughts 97
   Adopt Healthy Practices 99
   Reduce Stress 100
   Get a Good Night's Sleep 101
   Eat Healthy Foods 101
   Enjoy a Little Me-Time 102
   Know When to Seek Professional Help 103
   Chapter Summary 103

   Conclusion 107
   Appendix I 113
   Appendix 2 117
   Contributors 129
   Also Available from Parenthood Press 133
   References 135

INTRODUCTION

 Why fit in when you were born to stand out?

DR. SEUSS

If your child has just been diagnosed with autism and you feel lost, alone, or helpless, know that many children—in fact, one in every forty-four—are diagnosed with this condition (Autism Speaks, n.d.). The percentage of diagnosed children has increased dramatically over the last few years, but the numbers simply reflect the fact that children are being diagnosed at a younger age. It wasn't until the year 2006 that the American Academy of Pediatrics (APA) recommended that all children aged between 18 and 24 months be screened for autism during routine pediatric visits. As hard as coming to terms with the initial diagnosis can be, an early diagnosis is extremely useful. It enables you to become more informed about your child's condition, think about various therapies, and act quickly.

A diagnosis that brings big life changes is always difficult. Initially, you may experience feelings such as sadness, anxiety, or a sensation of being overwhelmed. Emotions can come in waves, with parents sometimes alternating between shock, disappointment, sadness, and a strong sense of relief. You may have this conflicting set of emotions yourself, despite having suspected that your child could have autism. Receiving a diagnosis is an affirmation of your suspicions, but it is also the spark you need to kickstart a proactive strategy. It means that you no longer have to be a passive bystander or hope that your child's challenging behaviors will go away on their own.

 He was 3½ [when diagnosed] but we already knew. The diagnosis was a relief, and we dove into getting the help that opened up for us. He's doing great!!

STEPHANIE WOOD

The decisions you make can have wonderful, positive, and life-changing effects on your child. Your journey will begin with reading and observing. Then, it continues with talking to professionals and other families of autistic children and gathering key information on what autism is and isn't. Children with autism have the same needs as other children. They need to be intellectually and socially stimulated. They can feel passionate about some subjects and less thrilled by others. They think, feel, and need love the way we do, but they express it in a different way. If you approach autism with a growth mindset, you can enthusiastically find ways to help your child learn, play, and better understand others and vice-versa. You will see "growth mindset" sprinkled throughout this book. Let's take a moment to understand what that means.

Dr. Carol Dweck created the phrases "fixed mindset" and "growth mindset" to characterize the fundamental assumptions people have about learning and intelligence after examining the behavior of thousands of children. Students understand that work makes them stronger when they believe they can get smarter. As a result, individuals invest more time and effort, which raises their level of achievement. For example, "I can improve my skills with effort and practice."

INTRODUCTION

If someone has a growth mindset, they embrace challenges and believe:

- Talents and intelligence can be cultivated
- Mastery is attained by effort
- Making mistakes is a necessary component of learning
- Failure is a teaching opportunity
- Failures are merely short-term setbacks

Let's begin by going over a few key facts about autism.

Millions of children are diagnosed with autism every year. If you consider how each child has many family members and friends in their lives, then it is easy to understand that nearly everyone is connected to this developmental disability in some way (Centers for Disease Control and Prevention, n.d.). Research shows that:

- Boys are four times more likely to have an autism diagnosis than girls.
- Autism can be reliably diagnosed at around the age of two, though most diagnoses in the US are made when a child is over four.
- Researchers believe that genetics are involved in the vast majority of autism cases.
- Children of older parents are more likely to have an autism diagnosis.
- Vaccines do not cause autism, as established by extensive research.
- Early intervention can improve a child's ability to learn, communicate, and interact with others. It can also aid in brain development.
- The most commonly used therapy for autistic children is Applied Behavior Analysis (ABA), which reinforces desired behaviors and discourages unwanted ones. This therapy is a

hot-button issue in the autism community and will be addressed later.

- Many children benefit from additional therapies such as speech and occupational therapy.
- Many young adults with autism do not receive healthcare for years after they stop seeing their pediatrician.

There are many more facts you will learn along the way, but the important takeaways from the findings above are that millions of people have autism, genetics seems to be the major player involved, early intervention works, and children need to continue to receive care as they transition into their teen years and adulthood.

PEGGY AND MIKE

When their three-year-old son, Jonah, was diagnosed with autism, Peggy and Mike said that one of the strongest emotions they felt was confusion. After a variety of tests, their doctor handed them information about local organizations and professionals to contact, but one of Peggy's biggest worries was the sense of not having control over her child's future. During her many visits to the clinic, she came to understand that worry, fear, and not knowing what to expect are normal reactions to the unknown.

In the beginning, it can be difficult to decide which course to take, which professional to see, or which therapy to opt for. When it comes to special needs, beginnings can always seem a little chaotic. Accept that it takes time to learn more about autism; speak to professionals, join parent support groups, and discover the latest scientific studies and recommendations.

Your child needs you to be their advocate, their warrior, and their greatest source of unconditional love. However, you can only begin to be all these things when you accept that autism is a complex disorder that will change the way you view essential aspects of your life. You can only feel empowered when you accept that sometimes you will have to experiment with different strategies and approaches before you find the right combination. Rather than feeling defeated, view unachieved goals as arrows pointing you in the direction you need to take. Switch up your plan when something doesn't feel right; let your instinct guide you as much as evidence-based practices and professional advice do.

> *My grandson was 3 when he was diagnosed. I somehow suspected it since he was about 6 months old (lack of eye contact, an unusual type of crawling, late walking), but his pediatrician denied it until I insisted on an evaluation. Knowing is half the battle. He is precious, special, and everything will be OK here as long as we know what to do and what is best for him! He is truly a blessing and very loved by his parents and grandparents. Such a sweetheart.*

DEBBIE ANDERSON

If you feel alone, try to expand your social circle. Building a solid support network is key, not only to your own happiness but also that of your family and your child. By meeting other parents, medical professionals, and therapists and embracing social situations instead of fearing them, you will start to understand that you aren't the only one going through this big life change. Good advice, humor, and friendship can all help pull you out of a slump when necessary, and having friends and family around gives you an assortment of important roles to fill.

Be vigilant for signs that you are not just sad but perhaps depressed. Symptoms to watch for include weight loss or gain, social withdrawal, sleep problems, and a loss of interest in the activities you used to love. See a therapist if you think you have depression or anxiety. As is the case with your child, the earlier you receive the help you need, the sooner you can view autism as just another fact of life that requires its own unique set of approaches.

INTRODUCTION

 My girl is 11. She is going to be tested at the end of the month. She was tested when she was little and they said she wasn't [autistic] but they wanted to redo it. She has severe anxiety and her sensory [issues] are insane. I'm having a really hard time with it. I don't know why I just want to cry. It just seems like it will be on paper and she will be "labeled" the rest of her life. That is the way I feel. Don't throw stones at me.

JESSICA BLAIR

It may take days, weeks, or months to find techniques that work, but the right approach for your child is there. This book will help guide you through the many approaches that have provided excellent results for many families. The good news is that we have decades of research on autism to guide us. We know the challenges, and we know what works. Through experimentation with different techniques and through consistency and commitment, you can achieve the positive results enjoyed by so many families across the globe.

This book highlights the importance of being as strong an advocate for your own health, happiness, and well-being as you are for your child. You are their rock, and you will continue to be important throughout their childhood, teen, and adult years. You may feel confused now, but you will soon look back and realize how incredibly resilient you are and marvel at how much you and your child have achieved. Autism does not define your child or your family. It's just a different way of processing life experiences, and many of the challenges it presents can be resolved with therapy, practice, and a solutions-focused, proactive attitude.

 Some days I do get moments where it makes me sad, but my son is happy and healthy and will show us the world through a different lens. I always try to look at his special abilities rather than his difficulties.

CLARE MCGOVERN

CHAPTER 1
AFTER THE DIAGNOSIS – WHAT NOW?

You will probably always have crystal clear memories of the moment you received your child's diagnosis because this news is life changing. In the hours and days that follow, you may feel overwhelmed by a flurry of thoughts and emotions, including the sudden realization that your life, hopes, and dreams have changed irrevocably. You may feel like running out of your doctor's office and slipping into bed to have a good cry or wish you were on a quiet mountaintop where you could let it all out and scream.

> Both of my kids were diagnosed 2 months apart: my son at age 2 and my daughter at age 4. It started a depression and anxiety that is still with me because I know how awful and ugly the world is when someone is so far different. I wish I could live forever because no one will love them like me after I'm gone.
>
> NICOLE CROSS-CLAY

Everyone handles difficult news differently, and you have your own unique way of processing challenging emotions. During these moments, repressing negative emotions or feeling guilty about having them is the worst thing you can do. You are entitled to feel fear, anger, disappointment, frustration, and worry. As you start meeting other parents and hearing their stories, you will discover that many initially feel exactly as you do.

 I just fished him out of a pond right before my brother's wedding...so [the diagnosis] wasn't a shock for me. Having said that, I assume all parents have a grieving period for a while.

TYLER MARTIN

Processing a diagnosis means understanding that your life is now different. What you may not realize at the time is that you will soon begin to develop new concepts of what happiness means for you, your child, and your family as a whole. There is no need to get everything right from the outset or to put up a tough front when you are feeling vulnerable. In the days immediately following the diagnosis, you should be vigilant about exercising the art of self-compassion, which simply means being as kind to yourself as you would be to anyone you love if they were going through a similar experience.

MARY AND JACK

Oscar had recently been diagnosed with autism. His parents, Mary and Jack, each took the diagnosis very differently. Jack's immediate reaction was one of immense relief. He was a football coach, and he faced challenges the way he would a tough game, by taking a solutions-based approach. For Jack, not knowing what was going on made him question his parenting, since he had tried so many approaches and was not managing to get Oliver to interact with him. Moreover, when he would talk to other people at work or at family get-togethers, they often thought he was simply making excuses for Oliver's behavior. More than one friend pointed out that their own children were well-behaved because of discipline and education. These words stung Jack, but because he didn't know about Oliver's condition, he wondered if he was doing something wrong or if he didn't have what it takes to parent Oliver well. His readings on child behavior seemed to suggest that Oliver could have autism. Jack had discovered, for instance, that Oliver had six of the eight autism traits listed on a leaflet about autism. He was fully expecting the pediatrician to simply confirm what he knew, and when this was the case, it was a real lightbulb moment for him.

Receiving a diagnosis also meant something else. Oliver now had access to the resources that would make a marked difference in his life. Early intervention is vital for autism, and it can have a big impact on a child's future capabilities.

For Mary, the experience was a combination of grief and shell shock. Although she knew that Oliver's development was very different from that of their older son, Sander, hearing the words "Yes, your son has autism" led her mind to jump to the future. A whole list of scenarios started playing out in her head, and she asked herself a barrage of questions. Would Oliver make friends at school? Would he be bullied? Would he be able to learn and succeed in his chosen profession in the future? Would teachers be supportive, or would they lose patience if he did not behave in a neurotypical way? What would everyone say? How would Oliver cope when they were no longer around?

Mary was worried that Oliver's autism diagnosis would pigeonhole her son and make others overlook his quirky sense of humor or his amazing abilities in math and languages. She did not want anyone to label him in a way that diminished him. She also wondered how this would affect Jack and Sander. Would it change the habits and routines they had spent years establishing? Sander was a curious and intellectual child who loved reading, watching documentaries, and cooking with Mary. She worried that he would be lonely if life suddenly changed and she had far less time to spend with him. Mary was also worried about work. She had a job she loved, and she wondered if she would be able to juggle her work obligations with the many appointments with therapists that Oliver would need. She wondered if she could rely on friends and family to lend a helping hand, and if not, would she have to leave her job? Would her family be able to get by on one salary alone?

As the weeks and months went by, Mary and Jack's reactions began to synchronize as they obtained early intervention services for Oliver and a wealth of resources became available to them. Mary began to develop new goals for Oliver and celebrated each small victory as though it were a championship match. Jack easily related to her ability to set goals and celebrate those achieved.

THIS IS THE SAME CHILD YOU HAVE ALWAYS LOVED

 My 8yo was 3½ [when diagnosed] and I already knew going in. I was sad in the beginning, but then I suddenly realized the diagnosis in no way changes who they are.

HOLLY MOLINA

As you begin to read more and develop a list of your favorite websites and blogs on autism, you will come across vastly different accounts of coming to terms with a diagnosis of autism. Blogger and educational consultant Megan Ashburn (Ashburn, 2019) didn't understand it when other parents told her to "give herself time to grieve" and "mourn." She learned that many parents are told by medical professionals and therapists to grieve, something she does not consider useful when it comes to a child who is very much alive. Ashburn states that although there is no right or wrong when it comes to how a person feels, it is important to question the reasons behind emotions so they can reframe their conversations. In her case, the array of emotions she experienced during her child's diagnosis included confusion, fear, loneliness, and disappointment. She makes a wonderful point. Disappointment is ultimately about *your* vision for your child's future. Your child hasn't actually changed because of a diagnosis. They are the same bright, bubbly, and curious child they were before you discovered they had autism.

 I didn't care [about the diagnosis] because my child was still the same child before the label as he is now after.

JULIANNE REGA

For more real, sometimes raw reactions from other parents, read more in Appendix 1.

CHILDREN WITH AUTISM ARE ACHIEVING GREAT THINGS

A large, longitudinal study by researchers from The Hospital for Sick Children and the Center for Addiction and Mental Health found that most children show proficiency or growth in vital developmental areas by the time they are ten years old (Szatmari et al., 2021). Instead of focusing on the children's deficits, the researchers used a strengths-based approach to obtain a larger-scale picture of how autistic children are doing.

Their results showed that the majority were doing well by the time they were in middle childhood. Moreover, some 80% of the participants had achieved growth or proficiency in at least one of five key developmental areas: (1) communication; (2) socialization; (3) activities of daily living; (4) internalizing; and (5) externalizing. Some 20% of the children did well in at least four out of five of the assessed skills by the time they were 10 years old.

In the study, the researchers pointed out one important issue: children with autism from racial and ethnic minority backgrounds and those from lower socioeconomic backgrounds are less likely to receive the same services their white counterparts do. Ensuring children receive necessary help early will help them have a more fulfilling life and thrive by the time they are in middle childhood. Information such as this can inspire you to advocate for equal access for all children to required services.

POSITIVE COPING STRATEGIES

If you are feeling sad or alone after your child receives their diagnosis, know that there are strategies that can help you develop a more positive outlook and feel more empowered (Rudy, 2021).

Read the *100 Day Kit for Young Children*. Autism Speaks *100 Day Kit for Young Children*, written for families of children aged four and younger, is meant to help you make the most of the first 100 days after the diagnosis. It is a good place to start, as it covers a wide range of topics, including the nature and signs of autism, understanding children's behavior, available treatments, and living with autism. It also has a week-by-week plan, which can help you kickstart your long-term strategy.

Give yourself time to accept the new circumstances. You may feel positive and energized one day and then a little disappointed the next day. For instance, a new therapy may not be working as well with your child as you had hoped. Sometimes, both sadness and joy may overlap. Accept the positive and negative feelings that come your way and, on your worst days, remember that these feelings are not permanent. None of them define you or your child. The emotions you feel can result from a myriad of factors, including how your day at work went, how much traffic you faced getting home, or whether you had an argument with someone earlier in the day.

Learn as much as you can about autism. Find out about exciting new therapies as well as tried-and-tested approaches. Slowly but surely, create your own list of techniques to try with your child. Do plenty of local research as well to discover schools, activities, and programs in your area that may be useful.

Set new goals and celebrate them. Your goal may be for your child to say, "I love you," or to look into your eyes and smile.

Remember the bonds you have already built with your child. When you start reading up on autism, you may want to immediately try a host of techniques, routines, and activities with your child. While proactivity is always a positive thing, do not lose sight of the little toddler or child you have always adored. Your number one role is as a parent, a person who provides your child's physical and emotional needs unconditionally. Always let the teacher or therapist in you take second place (Autism Speaks, 2016).

Avoid self-blame. There is nothing you did that caused your child to have autism. There is no room in your life for self-blame and self-judgment. Surround yourself with people who reaffirm your sense of self-worth. Avoid wasting energy on those who incessantly give unsolicited advice or who judge your actions or the behaviors of your child.

Don't let the diagnosis isolate you or your child. It is okay to take some time for yourself to read, recoup, and re-strategize. However, if weeks and months go by and you find that you are avoiding social occasions with friends and family, make an effort to build and reinforce these important bonds, even when it is the last thing you feel like doing. Try to recall the times you did not feel like making lunch or attending a Sunday barbecue. Nagged to attend by your family, you went anyway and ended up enjoying a great day out with new memories to cherish. Your family and social circle have a unique ability to make you feel like you are part of something bigger and stronger than yourself. They remind you that even in tough times, there is always something to laugh about.

Family and friends will be a vital source of support throughout your child's early years, teen years, and adulthood. They will be the ones you call when you feel like a weekend away, a long lunch, or a glass of wine while you watch the sunset. Regardless of the specific obstacles you may face, remember that having a happy life is about ensuring that all your needs, including those of love, friendship, physical health, mental health, and more, are sufficiently met. If you spend too much energy on just one of these, the rest will suffer, and you will lose the crucial balance you need to be the best parent, partner, friend, and family member you can be.

Give due importance to your other children. If you have other kids, speak to them openly about autism and ensure they feel like they can ask you any question in the world without you getting angry. When doubts arise, go to the internet and find the answers together. If you are still stumped by a subject, jot your question down and ask your child's pediatrician, therapist, or other health professional the next time you see them.

Be kind to yourself. Everything can seem worse when you're exhausted, haven't gotten enough sleep, or have encountered a conflict in your personal or professional life. On some days, it pays to let it go. Let excess energy out at the gym, enjoy a long bath or relaxing meditation session, give yourself the luxury of time reading a good book, and above all, try getting a good night's sleep so you feel refreshed the next day.

Enjoy your time together as a family. Your work week may be busy, but you should try to find a few fun moments together every day and make special plans on the weekend. Nature is a great stress reliever and a perfect backdrop for your child to enjoy the benefits of free play. As your child's advocate, you may be busy taking them to and from classes and therapies, but if you find that you need to set aside a specific time for winding down and simply being, then schedule it in. Autism should not stand in the way of all your favorite activities, be they outdoor sports, adventure sports, or visits to the homes of family and friends. Of course, you should also aim to make time to focus on your partner. Listen to their needs, opinions, and desires. Share your hopes and dreams with each other and try to schedule a date occasionally, relying on trusted friends or family members for babysitting duties.

ACKNOWLEDGING THE DIAGNOSIS

The *100 Day Kit for Young Children* reminds parents that there are four stages people usually go through after receiving an autism diagnosis. They are as follows:

1. **Awareness.** As families expand their reading material, watch videos on the subject, join forums, and begin to delve deeply into the subject of autism, they become more aware of the disorder and eventually share their knowledge with others.

2. **Acceptance.** Organizations, schools, families, and children themselves should be encouraged to see a person with autism as someone with many strengths and challenges. Autism should be approached with a growth mindset. The latter espouses that we are flexible human beings who are capable of changing, growing, learning, and improving. For instance, a child with autism may have challenges in the area of communication but may become an adult who enjoys expressing themselves and interchanging thoughts and ideas with others. Acceptance does not mean succumbing to defeat. Rather, it involves knowing the challenges you have and the tools you need to overcome them. It also means being proactive and flexible throughout your journey alongside your child.

3. **Appreciation.** This quality enables us to truly see and hear our children in all their perfect imperfection. Your child can give you gifts and memorable moments that are so beautiful, they are hard to describe to those who have not taken the time to really see them. Appreciation goes beyond your child. It should also extend to your partner, your other children, and the many friends and family members who make your life special. Perhaps one day your autistic child will leave the family nest, complete their college education, and embark upon an exciting professional life. When you look back and recall the very first day you received the diagnosis and you see

how far they have come, you will be filled with emotion and, most probably, a strong sense of nostalgia. All parents must work hard and overcome hurdles to help their children become their best selves. Parents of a child with autism may have to work a little harder in specific areas, but parenthood is always a beautiful mix of work, play, struggles, satisfactions, disappointments, surprises, and, above all, unconditional support and love.

4. **Action.** As you become your child's advocate, you will rely on a host of skills and support systems that will achieve goals such as self-determination, self-advocacy, independence, and social skills. When you stay focused, busy, and goal-oriented, you will feel the wonderful sensation of moving forward. You may have a setback or two. Don't let it stop you from moving, planning, and relying on evidence-based strategies and techniques. You will find the right set of tools you need to bring out the best in your child and enable them to enjoy a rich and happy life.

YOU CAN ONLY CHANGE YOURSELF

Your role as a parent is to help your child learn, play with others, and communicate their needs effectively, to name just a few goals. However, the aim is not to change your child. The only person you can truly change is yourself, and it helps to think about areas of your life that could benefit from having different priorities. When was the last time, for instance, that you worked out or prepared a healthy meal for yourself? How are your emotional regulation skills, and would you like to improve them? How well do you communicate your needs to your partner or your loved ones? Did you get more than seven hours of quality sleep last night? By valuing your own physical, mental, and emotional well-being, you can become the energetic warrior your child needs by their side.

You now have more information about how your child thinks, processes, and experiences the world. However, your child is the same person you have always known. Everyone has their own personality, tastes, dislikes, passions, and sense of style. The aim isn't to change anyone else but rather to help them express who they are and negotiate their way at school and in social settings.

SHARING THE NEWS

Autism is nothing to be ashamed of, and it most certainly should not be a secret. Bear in mind that one in forty-four children in the US has received the same diagnosis as your child. This means that many families will already know exactly what you are going through when you receive the diagnosis. Many will be eager to help, share recommendations, and give advice. In Chapter Five, we will delve more deeply into how to tell your family and close friends about your child's diagnosis.

It is, above all, important to share your news with your child when you feel they are ready and mature enough to have this important conversation (Delisle, 2021). One sign that your child is ready to learn about their diagnosis is when they start asking questions such as, "What is wrong with me?" "Why can't I be like my classmates?" or "Why is it so hard for me to make friends?" These inquiries are a clear indication that your child is ready for honest answers (Wheeler, n.d.).

It is logical to feel a little anxious about sharing the diagnosis with your child. You do not, by any means, want to negatively affect their self-esteem. Instead, you want to focus on empowerment, on seeing the diagnosis as a positive thing that will enable your child and your family to move forward. We mentioned how parents often feel a sense of a weight being lifted off their shoulders when they discover their child has autism.

It is much the same for children. Many may have spent years thinking that they were less valuable than their peers. It is reassuring for children to have a scientific, logical explanation that explains why they may struggle in a few areas. Receiving a diagnosis normalizes their disorder; it lets them know that they share key similarities with millions of children around them. As stated so eloquently by behavioral consultant Janet Arnold, self-knowledge is a prerequisite for self-esteem, self-acceptance, and self-advocacy. You need to know who you are before you can let your voice be heard.

WHAT SHOULD YOU TELL YOUR CHILD?

The extent of information you share with your child very much depends on the questions they ask. Start out with a simple explanation, talking a little about what autism is and the areas it affects. If you want to take a structured approach, consider looking at workbooks (Faherty, 2014; Vermeulen, 2012) that suggest specific steps to follow when telling your child about their diagnosis.

Remember Mary and Jack, who had very different initial approaches to their son Oliver's diagnosis? Mary is now a passionate, active advocate for her son; she tells a great story about how she shared the news of Oliver's diagnosis with him. She says that one day he was a bit cranky after school. While he was having his snack, he put his hands over his head and told Mary, "I don't know what's wrong with me. Nobody wanted to play with me today, and it's been this way all week long." Mary approached the beanbag where he was sitting, sat next to him, and said, "I think I know what is happening, and I have bought a few books that explain it very well." Mary had bought these books weeks before but had waited until the right time to share them. Inside each book, she had marked topics she thought might explain Oliver's specific struggles. She felt like she would burst with emotion when, looking through the pages, he said, "That's just like me!" Knowledge about his condition empowered Oliver, but it also let him know that he was not alone.

CHAPTER SUMMARY

A diagnosis of autism is not easy to take in, but for many parents, it can be a great relief. Strategies to adopt include:

- Give yourself time to adapt to the new situation and accept that you may feel sad, worried, or disappointed.
- Read as much about the subject as you can, so you can get your child started on a program that will help them improve in leaps and bounds.
- Share your news openly and with a view to teaching others about autism.
- Make it a point to meet many other people who have autistic children. Their support, reassurance, and guidance will help you feel supported, and your own strategies and plans for your child will soon help you understand that you are the best advocate your child could have.

CHAPTER 2

STRAIGHT TALK ABOUT AUTISM

A utism was once considered a somewhat mysterious condition that few people understood. This has led to incorrect beliefs and stereotypes that have been debunked over time. Whether you have a child with autism or are their teacher or loved one, it is important to educate yourself and dispel common myths that can cause harm and hurt a child's feelings. It is also important to understand that the autism spectrum is not linear, but spherical. Learn the correct language to use when talking about autism and be aware of the challenges you may face along the way.

WHAT IS AUTISM SPECTRUM DISORDER?

Autism Spectrum Disorder (ASD) is a developmental disability that can cause significant social, communication, and behavioral challenges (Centers for Disease Control and Prevention, n.d.). This means that autistic children may interact with others, communicate, and learn in ways different from most other children. Children with autism can range from gifted to very challenged in areas like learning and problem-solving. Because there can be great variation in symptoms among individuals, ASD is referred to as a spectrum disorder.

MYTHS SURROUNDING AUTISM

Among the many developmental disabilities that children can have, autism has been particularly plagued by false beliefs and myths (One Central Health, 2020). Do not be surprised if you encounter people who still believe these myths are true. While it is not your job to educate everyone you encounter, part of advocacy involves sharing your knowledge with those who have an open heart and mind. The information below can help you explain why the following beliefs are false:

- **Autism is a disease.** Children who have autism are not ill. Their brain simply works in a different way from other people. Autism is not a medical condition, and it has no cure, though autistic children may need support with some things. Finally, autism is not something that can be outgrown.
- **Vaccinations cause autism.** The myth that autism is caused by vaccines can be traced back to a dubious 1990 study that has since been debunked as deceptive, non-replicable, and non-indicative of the conclusion it came to. The researcher who published this study was subsequently stripped of his medical license. Unfortunately, the myth that there is a link between vaccines and autism has pervaded, and to this day, there are many people who make this false assertion. In recent years, study after study has shown that there is no link between MMR vaccines, for instance, and autism, even among children with other risk factors for autism (Hviid, 2019).
- **Children with autism don't speak.** This is another myth propagated by the media. While some autistic children can have delayed speech or use means of communication other than words, many have no speech issues. In fact, some may start talking earlier than their typically developing peers. Even if a child is unable to speak, they have the right to do so and they can be supported through strategies such as alternative and augmentative communication (AAC).

- **All people with autism have an outstanding savant skill or an intellectual disability.** People with autism have levels of ability that can vary across different skills and even within the same area. Some children do have exceptional abilities in some areas. However, around 66% of them do not have this type of ability. All children have their own strengths, and the best way to discover them is to get to know your child and to support their interests and passions. By the same token, it is wrong to assume that a child with autism has an intellectual disability, because many have an IQ in the typical or above-typical range.
- **People with autism do not experience the same emotions neurotypical people do.** Research has confirmed that people with autism feel the full spectrum of emotions. They may have difficulty expressing their feelings, but that does not mean they do not have them.
- **People with autism cannot form meaningful relationships.** People with autism do form strong, meaningful bonds with family, friends, partners, and children. They may find it difficult to understand social cues or express their emotions in a way that people understand. This is why developing an awareness of autism is key. Autism is not a one-way street. Although people with autism can benefit from learning how to interpret and display social cues, their loved ones should also make it a point to learn key skills and strategies.
- **Children with autism are aggressive.** As is the case with all other children, autistic children may scream or lash out when they are distressed, but this type of behavior is usually a communication of last resort. Children can learn the skills they need, and adults and loved ones can help by reducing sensory overload and other circumstances that can distress children with autism.
- **Autism rates are growing higher.** This myth demonstrates the importance of understanding the scientific method. It is not true that autism rates are rising dramatically. Current numbers simply show that more children today are being *diagnosed* than

in the past, and that is a good thing. It shows that awareness of autism is growing, and more parents are seeking a diagnosis and treatment. Greater awareness of autism is also important because it leads to wider-scale acceptance and understanding.

ARE AUTISTIC BRAINS DIFFERENT?

Autism is a neurodevelopmental condition that is diagnosed based on behaviors such as repetitive behavior, restricted social interaction and communication, and restricted interests. Research has not revealed a common brain structure that appears in all people with autism. However, there are trends among subsets of people with autism (Askham, 2020). For instance, children and adolescents with autism often have an enlarged hippocampus, the part of the brain that controls memory formation and storage. Some studies have shown that the size of the amygdala, the part of the brain primarily associated with emotional processes, differs between people who have autism and those who don't. People with autism can also have differences such as decreased brain tissue in parts of the cerebellum, a different pattern of thickness in the cortex (the outer layer of the brain), and altered white matter. In summary, while subsets of people can have the above or other brain differences, not all people do.

SIGNS OF AUTISM

Children with autism can have differences in the way they develop, the way they interact and communicate, the high-level skills they use, and their attention to detail. They may acquire skills at a different rate or in a different order than their neurotypically developing peers. For instance, they may be able to count to a high number but not be able to ask their parents for everyday items or greet others. They may recognize a wide array of words but be unable to read books.

In terms of social interaction, autistic children may have difficulty using eye contact and gestures to interact with others. They may not respond when their name is called or not notice the reactions and facial expressions of their classmates. They may also have different ways to show interest in things. For instance, instead of pointing at something they like, they might lead their parents to it. They may not engage in games like peek-a-boo or use hand gestures such as waving. They may also be less likely to share their interests, such as toys or books, with others. Role-playing games like pretending that they are caring for a doll may not interest them.

Children with autism may have difficulty understanding what others are saying to them, and they may find it hard to use language to express what they want to say (Healthline, n.d.). They may also not notice when someone is hurt, sad, or angry. They may also develop high-level skills, such as paying attention, organizing their work, time management, emotional regulation, flexibility, and adaptation, at a different rate than that of their peers.

Some children engage in stimming or self-stimulating behaviors (National Autistic Society, n.d.), which involves behaviors like repeating words, blinking repeatedly, rocking, rubbing or scratching skin, or rearranging objects. This isn't necessarily a negative behavior, because children can find it soothing, but it can potentially interfere with a child's quality of life or disrupt their work or play or that of their peers.

ARE THERE DIFFERENT TYPES OF AUTISM?

Today, it is typical to speak of autism as a spectrum. Until recently, however, it was common to talk about different types of autism, including:

- **Asperger's Syndrome:** This syndrome is essentially referred to as being on the milder end of the autism spectrum. A person with Asperger's may be highly focused and able to handle academics and work tasks but have more difficulties in areas like social interaction.

- **Pervasive Developmental Disorder:** This term was used for children who had more severe symptoms than those with Asperger's but less severe symptoms than those with autistic disorder.
- **Autistic Disorder:** An outdated turn for those with more intense or severe symptoms.

While these are out-dated terms, it pays to know their meaning in case someone around you uses them.

AUTISM: CAUSES AND RISK FACTORS

Much more is known about autism today than there was in decades past. We know, for instance, that there is no one single cause of autism (Autism Speaks, n.d.). Rather, it can arise from a combination of genetic and environmental factors. Known risk factors include:

- Genetics (autism tends to run in families)
- Advanced parental age
- Pregnancy and birth complications including extreme prematurity (birth before 26 weeks gestation), pregnancies spaced less than 12 months apart, and being a twin or triplet

Meanwhile, a decreased risk is associated with taking prenatal vitamins with folic acid.

COMMON INTERVENTIONS FOR AUTISM

There are various types of therapies and treatments for autism. Early intervention, which involves one or more of the following treatments, is important because it helps children learn key skills at a very young age. Common treatments include:

Cognitive Behavioral Therapy (CBT). This treatment encourages kids to understand the important connection between the way they think, feel, and act. The aim is to identify triggers for negative thoughts, emotions, and behaviors and to find a way to cope with them and respond with positive behavior.

Occupational Therapy. This treatment focuses on improving the skills kids need to make their way through daily life. Skills learned can include daily tasks like getting dressed and maintaining good oral hygiene, as well as the sharpening of fine motor skills.

Social Skills Training. The focus here is on teaching children how to read non-verbal cues and to start and engage in conversations, understand jokes, and show empathy for others' emotional states.

Medical Treatment. If autism is accompanied by or worsens another condition such as depression or panic attacks, medication may be recommended. Medication is only prescribed following a complete psychiatric evaluation.

Applied Behavioral Analysis (ABA). This treatment is a popular, although highly controversial, choice since it teaches children positive behaviors and encourages them to change negative ones. A trained therapist will work with your child and follow a structured plan. Skills learned include playing, communicating, and caring for oneself. ABA breaks down big goals into many individual ones, using repetition and encouragement to motivate children.

Despite the fact that studies have shown ABA to be effective, some parents and autistic self-advocates oppose its use. There are benefits and drawbacks to any treatment. The concerns on both sides are valid and deeply personal in some cases.

I loved it [ABA]. We had great therapists. They helped my child tremendously.

ANNABETT AVERY

The thing with ABA is that, at the core of the therapy, the goal is to have the autistic person blend in better with a neurotypical society. And that is wrong. There's no way of explaining that to be OK.

MARCELLA NOSTER

Huge NO from me.

KEILY J FAIRHEAD

For further, sometimes passionate discussion from a parent's point of view, read more in Appendix 2.

Using Assistive Technology. Technological devices and apps are making learning more fun and interactive for kids. Some, including Otsimo, Proloquo2Go, and Language Therapy for Kids–MITA, can be used on a smartphone or tablet, and they can teach children skills such as interacting with others appropriately via stories, photos, and other features that kids enjoy using (Carmen B. Pingree Autism Center of Learning, n.d.).

Alternative Therapies. As you do your research and interact with others, you may come across alternative therapies like hyperbaric oxygen therapy (lying in a chamber in which you breathe almost pure oxygen), chelation therapy (injecting a synthetic solution into the body to remove heavy metals from the body), but you should always check with your child's trusted medical team before trying out any new treatment.

UNDERSTANDING THE AUTISM SPECTRUM

A wonderful comic strip explanation of the nature of the autism spectrum (*The Art of Autism*, n.d.) shows exactly how mistaken people can sometimes be about what the autism spectrum is. People sometimes imagine that the autism spectrum looks like a straight line, with the words "not autistic" on one end of the line and the words "very autis-tic" on the other. Autism isn't linear at all. For instance, a child may find language confusing sometimes, and it may take longer to process conversations. However, they may enjoy starting and engaging conver-sations and simply take longer to respond. Yet, neurotypical people can also find language confusing; this quality is not, by any means, limited to people with autism.

When children hear words like "You're more autistic than I thought" or "I don't believe that this exercise makes you tired; everyone else is doing it," it can erode their sense of self, demotivate them, and make them feel like they are incapable of succeeding at anything. Words matter, and so does an understanding of the unique abilities and chal-lenges of each child, neurotypical or not.

The autism spectrum is spherical in nature, and it includes areas like motor skills, perception, executive function, sensory skills, and language. A child can have trouble processing information but have excellent motor skills. As *The Art of Autism* illustration shows, all people with autism have specific traits in different areas of the spec-trum. In some parts of the spectrum, a person will function no differ-ently from neurotypical people, yet they may still be affected by their environment. For instance, a child may enjoy taking part in conversa-tions but shut down when they are subjected to sensory overload, such as when a place is too crowded or loud. Another person may enjoy being at a loud concert but find it harder to take part in a conversation. Not all autistic people act the same way. Everyone has things that come naturally to them and others that are a bit more difficult.

It is also important to avoid using the term "high functioning." This term is not used by health professionals, researchers, or people with autism because it can be considered derogatory by others. The truth is that most people with autism function well in some areas but may need help in others.

Accomplished people who have autism are encouraging people to think twice before thinking of this condition in a linear fashion. Temple

Grandin, an immensely successful animal scientist and speaker, was considered low functioning as a child because she was non-verbal and she frequently screamed. The KISS special effects designer, who designed the rock band's fire-shooting guitars, was also underestimated in his childhood. Their experiences show that labels are not only meaningless but also capable of causing great harm to a child (Green, n.d.).

AUTISM VOCABULARY

Your autism-related vocabulary will undoubtedly grow exponentially as you start reading about the subject. Below are just a few terms that can kickstart your autism dictionary (We Rock the Spectrum Kid's Gym, 2020).

- **Discrete trial:** Breaking down tasks into smaller steps that are then put together to enable a child to perform a more complex task.
- **Echolalia:** The repetition of specific sounds, words, and phrases.
- **Joint attention:** The ability to share interests and activities with others. For instance, children may point at something or give another child a toy to encourage play. Autistic children may participate in little or no joint attention activities.
- **Perseveration:** Repeating an action after the stimulus that prompted it has stopped. It can also be described as becoming mentally stuck on something.
- **Scripting:** The repetition of words, phrases, intonations, or sounds, which can be taken from a book, film, or another type of media.
- **Sensory processing disorder (SPD):** A neurological condition that exists when sensory signals are inadequately processed. For instance, people with SPD can be highly sensitive to textures.

- **Splinter skill:** One or more skills your child may be particularly strong at.
- **Vestibular, or sensory system:** The system that makes us aware of balance and spatial orientation, which we need to perform coordinated movements. People with autism can have a harder time coordinating movements such as their gait.
- **Visual schedules:** Children with autism can benefit from using a visual representation of the tasks they need to carry out every day.

THE CHALLENGES OF RAISING A CHILD WITH AUTISM

Receiving a diagnosis of autism can do more than simply require you to reframe the plans you had for your child. It will also require extensive planning, especially with respect to care. A child with autism may have many therapy appointments to attend, and the school you feel is right for them may require you to travel a few more miles than you are used to. All this can take time to adapt to, and it can also put a stress on finances, especially if a parent has to reduce their hours at work or if they decide to leave their job to care for their child. It can be expensive to get around and pay for services, and the financial burden can be particularly heavy if families are not covered by insurance (Anand, 2021).

An autism diagnosis can also take a personal toll. Parents may find that they now have far less time for self-care or that they cannot manage to take part in the hobbies and pastimes that gave their lives meaning. Some couples can find that their relationship with their partner becomes strained as they struggle to come up with a plan that will enable their family to survive financially while providing the very best care for their child.

Stigmatization can be hurtful, and depending on who you encounter, you can feel accepted or judged. Not everyone is kind, empathetic, and accepting. You may hear snide remarks at a restaurant or receive a nasty look, and all these reactions can hurt you and your child. Unity and support are important buffers that will help you keep your bearings during challenging times. Sound financial planning, excellent time management skills, and even family therapy can all help you feel more in control of the situation, so you can be in the best frame of mind to pursue different options for your child.

PENNY AND KARA

Penny and Kara have an autistic son, Sam, now 30 and a computer programmer. When Sam was three, he had sensory issues that prevented him from being able to successfully learn toilet training skills. Penny and Kara were both busy lawyers at a family firm. Penny had decided to take a break from work because the couple had decided that Sam would receive full-time care at home until he was school-aged. Sam had numerous appointments throughout the week that one parent had to take him to. At one point, Sam's sensory issues resulted in constipation severe enough to require hospitalization. Due to the stress of the situation, Penny and Kara had an argument, all because Kara had arrived half an hour late to the hospital. By this time, Penny was exhausted and simply wanted a break. She also felt incredibly lonely, being suddenly cut off from her colleagues and having much less time to socialize with family and friends.

Penny and Kara had a tough couple of years, but once occupational therapy combined with applied behavioral analysis really began to click with Sam, the change in their dynamic was wonderful to see. It helped that Penny stopped thinking that her life had to be perfect. It took family therapy for her to discover that her career, health, and happiness mattered too, and that both she and Kara would have to compromise and commit to each other's, not just Sam's, well-being. In a way, Sam brought out the best in his family, teaching them the importance of patience and compassion and how to actively listen to each other.

When Sam turned five, Penny began working part-time. Penny's mother, a doting grandmother if there ever was one, took over a few duties, including taking Sam to therapy twice a week, and the couple was able to take advantage of their firm's flexible work schedule to do more work from home. This enabled them to save time on commuting and take part in the activities they needed to feel like their old selves.

Even in the toughest times, Penny spoke of Sam with love and often laughed from the heart while recalling some of the things he had said or done. She said that when, after many months of therapy, Sam finally mastered the art of potty training, he learned to celebrate with a little dance after his victory. Potty training is something so many families take for granted. For Penny, however, it revealed that although you may find parenting an uphill battle, when you look back at these child-hood memories, it all flies by so quickly, and if you could, you would do it all again in a flash.

CHAPTER SUMMARY

It is important to know the facts about autism so you know the specific challenges your child is facing. Be their staunchest ally by ensuring that you:

- Base your decisions on scientifically backed evidence.
- Know the most common myths surrounding autism, and how to debunk them.
- Know that autism is a spectrum. It is not linear.
- Learn all about both tried-and-tested and new treatments and therapies.
- Be prepared to come across people who get things very wrong, including those who think that autism is a linear phenomenon rather than the circular spectrum it actually is.
- Continue to read and update your knowledge throughout your lifetime. Autism will always teach you new, amazing things, even after your child is an adult in the real world chasing their dreams.

CHAPTER 3
PRIORITIZE YOUR CHILD'S SAFETY AND EDUCATION

An autism diagnosis is life-changing news that will require you to take a series of practical steps. In this chapter, we will focus on five key areas: (1) designing an autism-friendly home, (2) creating a financial plan, (3) embracing early intervention and different therapies, (4) accessing government and school services, and (4) advocating for your child.

HOME DESIGN AND SAFETY

Set Up an Autism-Friendly Home

If you are interested in home design, then you will enjoy the challenges and rewards involved in accommodating your home to your child's needs. Safety and comfort should be your top priorities, and although your child's activities and interests will change as they grow older, the following strategies can be helpful when you are designing an autism-friendly home for the first time.

Create an Appropriate Sensory Environment

Home interiors that are too cluttered with furniture, untidy, or that have too many loud or clashing colors and prints can overwhelm your child's senses. Human beings have a strong emotional bond with the visible light section of the electromagnetic spectrum. Colors can raise our heart rate and make us feel stressed out or have a soothing, calming effect. Recent research has shown that some of the most calming hues are navy blue, teal-like turquoise, and soft pastel pink. Green is also known to soothe the mind. Orange is associated with happiness and red with anger. Moreover, highly saturated tones stimulate and excite, while softer ones boost relaxation (IFL Science, n.d.).

Arrange Furniture According to Use

Avoid a cluttered design style and place furniture where it makes practical sense. If you have a workspace your child uses to do homework, make sure it has an ergonomic table-and-chair setup. The desk ought to have tidy drawers with the supplies your child needs for work that are clearly labeled. Desks and chairs should be placed far from high shelves or other objects that your child might be tempted to climb. Use pictures instead of written labels so that it is clear right away what each piece of furniture is used for. If your child's items are kept in storage boxes, choose transparent ones so your child can quickly find what they are looking for (Autism Society, n.d.).

Design a Quiet Spot for Your Child

If space permits, create a quiet space for your child to wind down. Use soft lighting and calming hues. Include plush items like cushions, bean bags, and soft toys. Remove anything sharp or hard from this area. Make sure the space is free of any odors or aromas that your child dislikes. If your child likes the smell of essential oils, place a diffuser in their room and use a relaxing oil like lavender.

Create Child-Friendly Spaces Throughout Your Home

Research indicates that a vast majority of adults with autism are not able to live independently, including those with higher IQs and those who received early intervention (Wang, n.d.). Teaching your child skills such as cooking, doing laundry, ironing, sewing, and similar household chores can all increase their likelihood of thriving in their own home.

In the kitchen, reduce the risk of burns by using an induction cooktop. Ask your electrician to install an automatic stove shut-off and use LED floodlights directly on workspaces so you can work comfortably. Consider having counters at a lower height for your child, and keep frequently used items at an accessible level. Let your child smell various herbs and spices; you may be surprised to find that they are very drawn to one or more specific herbs. Label items in these spaces and fit your home with non-slip flooring.

Finally, consider using natural materials like wood for everything from flooring to storage furniture, since these materials are known to have a calming effect. Include plants in your interior design scheme since these are known to relax adults and children alike.

Eliminate Injury Risks and Household Hazards

Ensure your home is child-friendly by covering electrical outlets with child safety plug socket covers and by using plastic knob covers on stoves, ovens, faucets, and doors. Lock the area where your washer, dryer, and power tools are located and cover all wires so that no accidents happen. You should also remove access to any items that could pose a danger to your child. These can range from toxic cleaning products to medication, scissors, staplers, lighters, and other similar household items. Lock the toilet tank cover so it does not fall on tiny toes.

Boost Your Child's Safety

Some autistic children can run away or leave the house without letting others know. This habit is known as "wandering" or "elopement." You can prevent this from happening by securing your home with a quality alarm system and fitting your windows and doors with locks. If your child has wandered in the past, contact your local police department and give them your child's details.

Take advantage of programs like Smart911 and Take Me Home if they exist where you live. Reach out to your neighbors as well, so they can notify you if they spot your child leaving your home.

Some children pound on glass in windows and other structures. If this is the case for your child, replace glass with a material like acrylic glass or polycarbonate panels, which are a combination of acrylics, polycarbonate, and other plastics and are virtually unbreakable.

Finally, you can consider purchasing wearable devices such as ID bracelets, cards, and GPS tracking devices. Role-play situations with your child in which someone might find them if they wander. This will ensure they are not alarmed when a helpful neighbor approaches to help them back home.

PREPARE FINANCIALLY FOR AUTISM

Autism costs families an average of $60,000 a year. This amount increases with the co-occurrence of intellectual disabilities. The costs come from medical health care, therapy, special education programs, informal care by friends or family members, lost work productivity, and other incidental costs.

Your child's needs may mean that a parent has to work less or give up their job, and currently, mothers are bearing the brunt of lost wages. They work less and earn 56% less than mothers of neurotypical children (Elemy, 2021). As a result, their families can have an income that is around $20,000 lower per year.

While most expenses are covered by insurance, parents still pay approximately $4,000 more in out-of-pocket expenses than families without children who have autism. Most autism-associated costs in the

US are for adults rather than children, though laws such as the 2014 Achieving a Better Life Experience (ABLE) Act allow states to establish tax-preferred savings accounts for people with autism and other disabilities.

When a member of your family is diagnosed with autism, it's crucial to run the numbers and weigh your options. If your home is a two-partner household, will it be more cost-effective to have one partner provide full-time child care or to hire a caregiver, even part-time?

Find and download the Autism Speaks *Financial Planning Tool Kit*, which gives vital information on aspects such as state and federal funding, special needs trusts, savings tools for people with disabilities, and where to obtain financial assistance if necessary. You should also consider seeing a financial planner, who can advise you on where to invest your money. Risk-averse parents of children with special needs may invest their money in secure options like insurance policies. However, in order for your funds to increase and subsequently sustain themselves over the long term, your financial advisor might advise investing some of your money in equity or other investment types. In order to properly plan your finances, you will need to identify your short-, medium-, and long-term objectives. This will take time and research. Your advisor can help you set up a trust, to which family and friends may wish to contribute.

With respect to health insurance, you should take out life insurance and opt for group insurance through your employer if this is possible, since this type of insurance covers your children. You can top this off with personal accident coverage for your child, which will protect them financially in the case of an accident or injury (Chakraborty, 2018).

Seek Financial Aid

In some circumstances, you could be entitled to financial assistance, including grants, government benefits, and loans. For instance, if either you or your child's other parent is receiving Social Security disability benefits, they may be eligible to receive Social Security Disability Insurance (SSDI). Most states also have medical waiver programs. These provide coverage for treatments, respite care, in-home aid, transportation, and more. You should call your local Community Action Agency, which provides assistance for low-income people and can help in the case of emergencies. For advice on affordable housing, contact the Department of Housing and Urban Development (HUD). USA.gov has comprehensive information on various types of government assistance.

The Family and Medical Leave Act

The Family and Medical Leave Act (FMLA) allows you to take unpaid leave from your job for up to 12 weeks to care for a child with autism. The Act does have specific requirements, such as the requirement that your employer be covered by the Act. Specifically, they have to be located within a 75-mile radius of your home and have at least 50 employees. State medical and leave laws may apply to employers in some states with fewer than 50 employees. You must have worked 1,250 hours or more in the US or a US territory during the previous 12 months in addition to being on your employer's payroll for at least 12 months (U.S. Department of Labor, n.d.).

EARLY INTERVENTION AND THERAPIES

The ages of birth-to-three are considered critical in terms of child development, so it is important to investigate different therapies for your child as early as possible. Gather a team of doctors and therapists and update them on your child's progress. The team can include pediatricians specializing in developmental behavior, gastroenterology, biomedical interventions, autism, and general practice pediatricians. Remember that your child can have other medical issues, and it is essential to have all the usual checks, such as tests for vision, hearing, and similar screenings.

You might also consider adding a biomedical expert to your team (Ali, 2015). Food sensitivities, nutritional deficiencies, gut and brain inflammation, gastrointestinal issues, allergies, and other issues can be linked to autism. Biomedical experts may recommend alternative treatments like B12 supplementation, anti-inflammatory treatments, and a gluten-free or casein-free diet.

Your team will also probably include one or more therapists, including physical therapists to help with gross motor skills, occupational therapists for fine motor skills and stimming management, and speech therapists for challenges with language and communication.

We mentioned previously that ABA is one of the most commonly used therapies for autism, but there are many more. Floor time, which involves parents playing on the floor with their children to meet them at their developmental level, is one of them. Another is the Picture Exchange Communication System (PECS), which involves the use of cards with images, words, or symbols rather than speech to help children with autism communicate while their speech is developing.

Then there is verbal behavioral therapy. This is based on ABA and involves connecting words with purposes, so children learn that words can get them the things they want.

Consider reading more about sensory diets. An organized schedule of activities known as a "sensory diet" is given to a child in order to help with their attention span, level of arousal, and ability to respond in a healthy way. Based on the theory of sensory integration, the activities are selected to meet the needs of that particular child.

It is important to take a positive approach and be willing to try different methods until you get to know your child and their preferences better.

You should also aim to stay abreast of new developments and scientific studies. For instance, a new therapy for infants can lessen the likelihood that they will be diagnosed with autism before they reach school age, according to research conducted in September 2021 at the University of Western Australia in Perth under the direction of Professor Andrew Whitehouse (Sample, 2021). Children who showed early indications of potential autism, such as not responding to their names or avoiding eye contact, were treated with this therapy. The goal of the therapy was to enhance parent-child communication.

Access Government Services and School Support

The Individuals with Disabilities Education Act (IDEA) entitles children with disabilities such as autism to access an array of free or low-cost services (Help Guide, n.d.). These include medical evaluations, speech therapy, physical therapy, parental counseling and training, assisted technology devices, psychological help, and more. A child younger than ten years old will not need a diagnosis of autism to obtain these services. If they have any delays, such as in social development or communication, they are automatically entitled to them.

Early Intervention Services (From Birth to Two Years)

Babies and toddlers are entitled to take part in an early intervention program. Your child undergoes an evaluation, and if a developmental issue is found, you work alongside early intervention staff to formulate an Individualized Family Service Plan (IFSP). This plan outlines your child's needs and the services they will receive. Your child's IFSP can include various therapies, such as speech and physical therapy, all of which aim to enable your child to transition well into school. Your pediatrician will usually refer you to early intervention services, but you can also call support organizations and the Autism Society National Helpline for further information.

Special Education Services (Ages Three and Older)

Children of this age receive individualized assistance via school-based programs. Children with autism are sometimes placed in classrooms with other children who require individualized assistance, though they may spend part of their day in a classroom with neurotypical children. Parents wishing to access these services must ask the local school system to evaluate their child so an Individualized Education Plan

(IEP) can be created. This plan stipulates goals to be achieved for the school year and indicates the type of support or service your child will receive. It is important to understand that the IEP is not set in stone. If at any time you feel your child has needs that are not being addressed, you can request an IEP meeting. You can also disagree with recommendations, seek an external evaluation, and ask anyone you wish, including family members or health professionals, to be part of the EIP team.

Should You Set Up a 504 Plan?

A 504 plan is covered under Section 504 of the Rehabilitation Act, a federal law that protects people against discrimination because of their disability (Schmidt, n.d.). This type of plan provides support and accommodations but does not list goals like an IEP does. It is reviewed every three years, though parents can request an earlier review if they wish. A 504 plan covers people with disabilities that substantially limit their life activities. They are often granted to students who may not require specialized teaching but who do require social or behavioral support.

Whether or not you opt for an IEP or a 504 plan depends on the needs of your child. For instance, if your child has autism and is doing well academically but may need help with social skills, then a 504 plan may be ideal. On the other hand, if your child's disability is adversely impacting their education, then an IEP may be the better choice (School Psychologist Files, n.d.). Study both options well and consult your school's special education teachers before making your choice.

Extended School Year (ESY) Services

If there is evidence that there has been a substantial regression in your child's skills during vacation time, they may be entitled to ESY services, which are provided over long breaks like the summer season.

Your Child's Rights to Assistive Devices

If your child's IEP team determines that your child requires assistive devices to benefit their education, then the school district is obliged to provide them. When you have an IEP meeting, insist that these devices be stipulated in writing as part of the plan. The district cannot deny the provision of assistive devices because of cost or a lack of staff training. If the IEP determines that your child needs to take one or more devices home to help them advance in their educational goals, then your child will be able to do so. Remember that you have a voice and that you can disagree with respect to the school's decisions regarding assistive technology.

Assistive technologies that can benefit a child with autism (Rudy, 2021) range from low-tech devices (devices that do not require electricity, like picture boards or a weighted vest) to mid-tech devices (such as battery-operated sensory toys) and high-tech devices (like augmentative communication technology). These technologies can help in areas such as communication, learning, executive functioning, social skills, sensory goals, and more.

What About Private Schools?

The majority of autistic children attend public schools, but there are different environments within the public system. These environments can range from classes with support to classes for all special needs, from public autism classes with some mainstreaming to public autism classes without mainstreaming (Rudy, 2022). Public education has several advantages, including the fact that it is free and that autistic children can receive individualized learning plans. The cons are that, depending on your district and other matters, the school your child attends may not have the budget to enact specific plans or achieve all your goals. You may not be happy with the school's approach; your child may find that sensory challenges within a typical school setting are overwhelming, or bullying may arise.

Private schools can be beneficial in terms of creating the right sensory environment for your child and offering specific programs that are autism centered. However, some parents prefer the public system because it enables their children to interact with a wider array of children and adults, thus helping them pick up skills they may need when they graduate. To check out what private schools can offer you, check out the websites of schools like the Carrie Brazer Center for Autism & Alternative Approaches in Miami, New Hope Academy in Illinois, or the Behavior Analysis Center for Autism in Indiana (The Best Schools, 2022).

BEING YOUR CHILD'S ADVOCATE IS A LIFETIME JOURNEY

Being your child's number one advocate is a lifelong goal that will require different skills depending on their needs. In addition to researching, you can make the best decisions for your child by speaking with autism specialists for further evaluation. Many top professionals can be found via local or state organizations in your area. Advocacy involves various actions, including:

- Placing your child on waiting lists for education services if necessary
- Learning about the legislation that covers your child's needs, such as the Individual Disabilities Act
- Knowing about your child's rights to a free appropriate education

 I was upset and in shock [about the diagnosis] but I vowed then I was going to do anything and everything I could for her. Today she is 11 years old and in middle school in an accelerated program so that by the time she receives her high school diploma she will also receive a college degree at the same time.

CAROL HINCH

Following the Seven Principles of Advocacy

Areva Martin, author and mother of a child with autism, identifies seven key principles that are helpful when it comes to ensuring your child gets the attention, support, and assistance they need to thrive in their childhood and adulthood (Dower, 2013). These are:

1. Take on a leadership role. Be a proactive parent who meets confidently with doctors, teachers, therapists, and everyone who plays an important role in your child's life.
2. Become an expert. Reading, networking, and speaking to other parents will help you become a specialist in your child's needs.
3. Think critically. As a parent of a child with autism, you may be presented with a host of information from different sources. Rely on evidence-based approaches to make the best decision for your child.
4. Speak authoritatively and be proactive. Read up on autism and practice and learn what you want to say at IEP and other meetings. Back up your statements with evidence.
5. Bring useful documentation to meetings. This can include medical reports, notes taken during meetings, and a journal recording your child's experiences.
6. Be a team player. Ensuring your interactions with others are high-quality, respectful, and solutions-focused will make others look forward to working alongside you.
7. Educate others. Accept the chance to educate others in your community about your child's condition. Explain the ins and outs of autism to your friends and family in a compassionate, understanding manner. Remember that many people lack an awareness about this subject and that by sharing your knowledge with patience and kindness, you can make a real difference.

CHAPTER SUMMARY

Being a parent of a child with autism requires you to learn, speak up for your child, and make important choices about your child's education. In no time, you will have detailed knowledge not only of autism but also of your child's specific needs. Remember that:

- You are your child's staunchest and most valuable advocate.
- There are many ways you can make life easier for your child. Start by designing an autism-friendly, safe home.

Make it a point to:

- Prepare financially for autism and discover any financial assistance and government assistance your child may be entitled to.
- Consider whether an IEP or a 504 plan is most suited to your child's needs.
- Read up on your child's rights, including their rights to assistive devices.
- Be confident and speak up when your child has needs that aren't being met.
- Expect a few setbacks along the way and come up with creative solutions.

Remember the value of educating others with an open heart. Know that through your teachings, patience, and kindness, you can make a big difference in the way others view autism and your child.

CHAPTER 4
LIVING WITH AUTISM

I n addition to making major decisions about schooling, therapies, and finances, managing day-to-day relationships is also important. This chapter will focus on your daily interactions with your child and on ensuring that everyone in your home feels supported, loved, and understood. We will delve into practical matters such as record-keeping but also cover areas such as helping your other children adjust, having a structured environment, helping your child with visual tools, and understanding your child's behavior and struggles. We will also reveal how behavior intervention training for parents can help you learn useful strategies for coping with challenging behaviors and identify some of the struggles your child may come up against in their daily life.

KEEP RECORDS AND ORGANIZE YOUR FILES

It is important to keep accurate, organized records, as you never know when an important document may be required or when your partner or your child's siblings may need access to information while you are out of the house. You should ideally store as much information on the cloud as you can. Share important documents or folders with family members and any professionals you wish to have access to this information.

Any information available in paper form should be filed away in one or more clearly labeled folders, which you can arrange by subject, date, or whichever way you find most useful. Some of the most useful records you will need to keep include diagnostic information, evaluations, progress reports, and IEPs (Operation Autism, n.d.).

For your filing system, you can divide records into two folders: one for current records and another for archived records. Use subject dividers, for instance: IEP, Evaluation, Progress, and similar. In the second folder, use the same dividers and different clear pockets for each subject. When you get a new IEP, get the old one and put it into the second folder inside the IEP divider, indicating the year of the document on the pocket so you can easily find it in the future. Keep the newest pockets on top so that everything is in chronological order. You can create a similar system for digital records using tools like Dropbox or Microsoft OneDrive.

SUPPORT YOUR OTHER CHILDREN

If you have other children, they will also need to know about their sibling's diagnosis and how to deal with and help with certain behaviors. As is the case for parents, the more informed children are about autism, the more they will know what to expect and the easier they will adjust to necessary changes. Explain what having autism means in an age-appropriate way. Give them specific examples of how they might need to interact with their sibling and identify and manage their negative feelings when these arise.

Provide them with books, videos, apps, and other resources so they better understand their sibling's diagnosis (Autism Speaks, n.d.). The Organization for Autism Research (n.d.) has resources for parents, teenage siblings, and young children. These can be downloaded for free online.

Children should be free to feel angry, hurt, or even jealous that parents are spending so much time and effort on another sibling. They should feel free to express their emotions without fear of judgment, but also be reassured that they are just as loved as their sibling with autism and that they are a vital and loved member of your family.

Parents can help their children by teaching them to identify different emotions and finding healthy outlets for them. When siblings are stressed, for example, techniques like deep breathing, spending time in a forest or nature-filled zone, and meditating can all help them ride through a difficult moment instead of reacting with anger. Children who are well-informed and who feel loved and supported at home can make excellent advocates for their siblings with autism. To ensure this is the case, consider the following strategies:

- Join a sibling support group and/or an autism family support group. Your kids will love meeting other children their age who are adapting to the same challenges (Raising Children, n.d.).
- Set family rules that are fair and consistent for all of your children.
- Give everyone their own set of chores, including your child with autism.
- Try not to accept aggressive or hurtful behavior from any of your children. Teach them ways to express negative emotions and reward good behavior.

CREATE A STRUCTURED HOME ENVIRONMENT

Structured home environments set expectations and create order for everyone at home, and consistency is particularly important for autistic children. Predictable routines help them feel safe, since sudden changes and not knowing what to expect can be overwhelming and frustrating. These emotions, in turn, can lead to challenging behaviors such as meltdowns and tantrums. A structured lifestyle can also help children develop better sleeping habits and regular eating patterns, and it can promote an overall better mood.

Having a structured home does not mean you have to be rigid. It can simply provide the answers to questions like "Where do the crayons go when you are done playing with them?" "What containers do you keep your toys in?" or "What do you do with your clothes when you get ready for bed?" An important part of creating structure involves giving children clear expectations. While every home has its own set of routines, you will find a few ideas below that may help you establish a positive structure.

Use visual tools to establish routines. Children with autism tend to prefer learning things visually rather than verbally. The Picture Exchange Communication System (PECS) is just one system that uses symbols and images to supplement language. You can use pictures to show a child what you want them to do, and you can try using a timer, which can help your child know how much time they have for a specific activity. You can also use visual timetables with pictorial representations of the sequence of activities for the day. For instance, when your child wakes up, you can say, "Now we're going to have breakfast, then we're going to get dressed, then we will get in the car and go to school." You can point to the different pictures as you say this and as you transition from one activity to another (Ambitious about Autism, n.d.).

You can also use "Now and Next" templates, which have two columns: a "Now" column and a "Next" column. You can place a photo of the activity you want them to do now, such as brush their teeth, in the "Now" column, and place the subsequent activity in the "Next" column. You can use this template to motivate your child to do something they are not so excited about. By putting a fun activity in the "Next" column, they will most likely complete the more arduous "Now" task willingly and in a quicker fashion.

Label drawers and other storage furniture. This will ensure that your child always knows where to find useful materials and toys.

Organize items. Have lots of compartments or dividers for different categories of items. If you keep your child's toys in clear boxes, place soft toys in one box, cars in another, blocks in another, and so forth. Do the same with clothing, eating utensils and glasses, and any other items your child uses regularly.

Respect regular times for activities such as doing homework, taking a shower or bath, having dinner, brushing their teeth, and sleeping. If your child is older, they can have a list of chores, which can include tidying up their toys, setting the table, and washing or drying the dishes. The chores you choose should be appropriate for your child's age and skill level. Some routines can be completed even by young children. These include throwing away food wrappers, cleaning up after playtime, putting their dirty laundry in a basket, and bringing their plate or glass to the sink after they are done with it. Make sure your child's bedtime routine is structured, so they can enjoy good sleep quantity and quality. At nighttime, you might read them a story before turning off the light.

When establishing a new routine, remember that it can take time for children to get used to it. Be consistent, keep using visual supports as long as you need to, and praise your child when they complete key steps. Occasionally, add components to the routine, such as flossing after brushing. While structure is important, so too is being flexible. As your child grows and matures, their routine may change slightly or require additional steps.

UNDERSTAND YOUR CHILD'S BEHAVIOR

Your child may have challenging behaviors, and you can deal with them better if you know their triggers and causes of stress. When you know the causes of specific behaviors, you can help replace them with more constructive ones by following the strategy that works best for your child.

Children with autism can occasionally display aggressive or inappropriate behavior. They can refuse or ignore requests and hurt themselves or others. They can also show behaviors that others may consider unusual, including avoiding eye contact and fidgeting. Sometimes, children adopt these behaviors to help themselves feel better. For instance, fidgeting is simply a way of using movement to help them concentrate, and it can be an outlet for nervous energy. Such is the usefulness of fidgeting that there are now specially designed objects called "fidgets," which look like toys but actually have therapeutic benefits. Fidgets can be anything from a squishy ball to putty, therapy bands tied to chair legs, and small cubes with many different buttons that children can press (Pacer, n.d.). On the other hand, avoiding eye contact may be a way for kids to stay calmer and more focused. Forcing a child out of these behaviors may actually make paying attention and/or conversing more difficult.

What Can Trigger a Child to Adopt Challenging Behaviors?

There are many reasons why your child may be having a difficult time on a given day. For instance, they may have sensory difficulties, and the noises, lights, and other stimuli that most people filter out may be incredibly physically and emotionally draining for your child. When your child feels overwhelmed by sensory stimuli, they may stim (rock, jump, headbang, or spin), talk faster and louder, cover their ears, or chew on things. They may even have difficulty recognizing needs such as hunger or the need to use the bathroom, or they may have a meltdown.

Your child may also simply be tired or struggling to make a transition to a new school, classroom, or teaching approach. They may find it hard to meet goals that are simply too difficult for them at a given time. Unfamiliar or unpredictable social situations, changes to their everyday routine, difficulties interpreting others' thoughts or feelings, and even their own worries can cause stress.

Be on the Lookout for Signs of Stress

Because your child may not be able to communicate what is bothering them, you need to be sensitive to their reactions in order to find the cause of their stress. In addition to engaging in some of the behaviors mentioned above, such as stimming, your child may show more subtle signs of stress. These can include insisting that routines be followed, having sleep issues, withdrawing from social situations, relying more on rituals such as lining objects up or spinning them, and scratching or biting skin.

DEAL WITH YOUR CHILD'S BEHAVIOR

Dealing with challenging behavior starts with observing your child for triggers. Use a journal or diary (Raising Children, n.d.) and write down the following:

- The challenging behavior
- The time and place it happened
- What the situation was before the behavior happened
- What occurred after

An example of challenging behavior could be your child hitting a sibling in the car. The behavior could have started because when you picked your child up from school, you had to stop at the store to buy dinner. When your child started hitting their sibling, you briefly tried to soothe your child, then went home. In this situation, the trigger could be an interference with their normal routine. If you usually drive straight home, your child could be upset by the fact that you took a different route.

Make Changes

Once you know what happened, you can take steps to make changes. For instance, you can use visuals, such as a picture of the store, so your child knows where they are going. If you know you need to go to the store beforehand, you can use a social story with three different images saying, "First, Mom will pick you up, then we will stop at the store, then we will go home."

You can also aim to reduce the likelihood of sensory overload by choosing a quiet time to shop or by going to a place that has toys or treats your child likes. Bring along an item that gives your child comfort, such as their favorite soft toy.

When explaining where you are going or what you are doing to your child, don't give too many instructions. Stick to one idea at a time. Let your child know they can ask you for help when they need it. They could simply say "help" or hold up a sign saying "help."

When your child is protesting about something you must do, try to calmly ignore them. When they do display positive behavior, give them plenty of praise. Try different reward methods. Some children find classic sticker charts motivating.

Use Clear Communication

When your child displays challenging behavior, direct them to a positive alternative behavior instead of telling them what they shouldn't do. For instance, if they pull a crayon out of their little sibling's hand, tell them, "Wait until Nicky is finished before taking that color."

Teach Your Child Self-Calming Techniques

Strategies such as deep breathing while thinking of something they love, reaching out to an adult for a hug, going to a calm corner, or listening to or singing a preferred song can all help soothe a child who is having a meltdown. Experiment with different methods (Morin, 2021) until you find a select number of them that work particularly well with your child. These can include:

- Have a sensory box. Stock this box with items like fidget spinners, squeeze balls, things to chew on, and similar toys. Personalize this to your child and their preferences.

- Teach your child an escape plan. For example, you can set up a calming space at home that your child can seek refuge in if they are feeling stressed or anxious.
- Learn meditation techniques. Meditation is a powerful way to lead a child out of an anxious state. There are many apps catered specifically to children. Some provide fun activities that evoke imagery and characters that children can relate to. Just a few apps you might look into are *Headspace for Kids*; *Stop, Breathe & Think*; and *Calm*. Children who enjoy meditation may also like yoga, which is another powerful stress-busting activity.
- Create calming routines. The book *Active Imagination* has excellent sensorimotor activities that are specifically aimed at helping children improve their focus and attention.
- Try distraction. Some parents find that a child who is distressed can suddenly become fully immersed in a video of animals, kids' characters, and the like.
- Keep your kids active. Kids who are physically active can find their favorite sport to be an excellent way to expend excess energy and let loose the day's accumulated tension.
- Have a pet. Pets are known to benefit the mental health of those who love them, and a recent study (Carlisle et al, 2020) has shown that they can be a big source of comfort for autistic children and their parents. Pets have a unique ability to encourage social interaction while simultaneously decreasing anxiety.

Seek Professional Help

If you have tried various strategies and find that you are still having major difficulties, know that help exists. Seek recommendations for a good child psychologist or developmental-behavioral pediatrician, since these professionals are ultra-focused on behavior, and they can suggest new strategies in line with their research and experience.

INTERACT WITH YOUR CHILD

When interacting with your child, know what to expect (University of Rochester Medical Center, n.d.). Children with autism:

- May not be able to understand non-verbal communication such as a frown or a smile
- May take words literally
- May not be able to handle too many thoughts or instructions at once
- May want to keep the topics of conversation to areas they are interested in
- May become overwhelmed by everyday textures, smells, sights, sounds, and tastes
- May use nonverbal communication methods such as taking a person's hand and bringing them to something they want, pointing at something then looking at a person to let them know they want it, or handing an object to someone to communicate

To communicate effectively with your child, try to maintain a calm, positive, yet curious stance. Learn to listen with your eyes as well as your ears, since everything your child does is trying to tell you something. Use short sentences. Use clear language and change your tone of voice to emphasize specific words. For instance, you might say, "Wow, that snowball is VERY cold." Get your child to engage in communication by asking them questions that need answers, like "What did you have for lunch today?" or "What did you do at playtime?" Give your child time to give you their answers and focus on topics they like talking about.

Teach your child to express negative emotions like anger or frustration in an assertive but not aggressive manner. When your child acts out, try to ignore their behavior, giving them plenty of attention when their behavior is positive. Be willing to learn from your child, and let a

sense of humor and a sense of enjoyment prevail in your daily interactions.

SUPPORT YOUR CHILD'S GROWTH

Ensure your child enjoys a wide range of fun, entertaining, educational, and cultural experiences (Meduri, n.d.). Below are just a few
ideas that can help them have a fun, rich life filled with different
activities:

- Organize play dates and sign them up to a social skills group.
  Try to meet up with kids who share the same interest as yours
  and choose an activity or place you know your child loves.
  This could be the park, skating rink, or the beach. Avoid noisy
  places or those that are overcrowded and time your visit well.
- Sign your child up for their favorite sport. If they enjoy
  competition, they may be interested in a program like Little
  League Challenger Division, TOPSoccer, or similar team
  sports.
- Let your child's talents shine through. Support them by
  making it easy for them to spend time on their favorite hobbies
  and interests.
- Teach them life skills such as self-kindness, pursuing your
  interests, being an advocate, educating others on autism,
  building social relationships, and even earning a living by
  doing something they love. An older child who would love to
  start a business, for instance, may enjoy learning how to make
  a business plan, make their product, and market it.
- Give them plenty of learning opportunities. Structured play,
  sensory play, and unstructured play can all help your child
  develop different skills. Make learning fun by including
  entertaining, hands-on activities such as making scented
  playdough, setting up a car wash station for their toy cars,
  setting up a mud kitchen, painting with hand and footprints,
  blindfold food tastings, and making different colored slime.

IDENTIFY AND DEAL WITH COMMON STRUGGLES

Children with autism can find situations they may encounter on a day-to-day basis difficult to process. We mentioned the importance of rituals and delved into how changes to a child's routine can make them upset. Something you might see as a small change, such as reading in a different spot, going to a friend's house on a Friday night, or asking someone else to pick up your child at school, can be confusing and distressing. The use of social stories, giving a child extra time to calm down, and encouraging a child to try out self-calming techniques can be helpful.

A child can also struggle with being left out. To ensure they feel loved, accepted, and sought out, treat them the same as you do their siblings, let them know they are always invited to social events, take them with you as you undertake your daily activities, and adapt the way you communicate. For instance, if your child does not like answering questions, simply make comments that show you are interested in what they are doing (Kelly's Thoughts on Things, n.d.).

Prepare for Puberty

Puberty is always a bit of a tough stage, as teens and adolescents can be impulsive, and many teens find it hard to regulate their emotions or read others' non-verbal language since their brains are still developing. Share interesting facts about puberty with your child. Let them know it is normal to feel a little confused at times. Teach them about the importance of privacy and the difference between appropriate and inappropriate touching.

Address Bullying

People with autism can be at a higher risk of being bullied by their peers because they can find it difficult to read facial expressions and body language (National Autistic Society, n.d.). Be vigilant for signs of bullying. These include your child coming home with torn or dirty clothing, arriving home late because they have changed their route to avoid bullies, asking to stay home from school, seeming stressed or depressed, displaying more repetitive behavior more intensely or frequently, and doing worse on academic assessments.

If your child is involved in bullying, either because they are being bullied or because they are bullying others, speak to your child's teacher or school and find out what strategies they propose. The school may also suggest practical things you can do or tell your child to improve the situation. Write down what you agree upon and send a copy to the teacher or school. Make sure to contact them regularly to ensure improvements are being made.

RECEIVE PARENTAL TRAINING IN BEHAVIOR MANAGEMENT

Improving your own skills via parental behavior intervention can be very fruitful for your child and yourself. A trial study published in JAMA (Bears et al., 2015) showed that training parents in techniques for managing behavioral issues can reduce the frequency of these problems. In the study, parents of autistic children received this training over eleven sessions lasting sixty to ninety minutes each. The results showed that the children of these parents made significant behavioral improvements compared to children whose parents had not participated in this type of training.

Adjusting to a life with autism involves observing, adjusting, and acting. The early days can be a challenge for parents until they establish clear routines, work out which strategies work best with their child, and, of course, ensure that your other children continue to feel loved, supported, and part of a unified family team.

CHAPTER SUMMARY

Living with autism can sometimes feel like juggling many balls in the air, but you can soon turn your home into a well-oiled machine by following these useful strategies:

- Organize your child's files in such a way that you can easily find everything you are looking for.
- If you have other children, make sure their needs are cared for and make sure they have quality time with you.
- Create structure and follow a routine at home, using visual tools to make the process easier.
- Identify your child's triggers and use calming strategies to soothe them when they are stressed.
- Use clear language to communicate with your child.
- Seek professional help if you have tried various strategies and are still dealing with major behavioral problems.
- Support your child's growth and friendships by ensuring they have a wide range of social events to attend.
- Get ready to talk about important aspects of adolescence with your child when they hit their teen years.
- Be on the lookout for signs of bullying.
- Consider parental training in behavior management so you can access a wide range of tools and resources.

CHAPTER 5

YOU DON'T HAVE TO DO THIS ALONE

Building a support system is critical when you have a child with autism. The number of responsibilities and the demands on your time and energy, not only from your child but also from other members of the family, can cause you to burn out if you don't take active steps to avoid it. You may not be the only one who needs support in your family. Your partner or your other children may also need to form part of a safe group in which they can share their thoughts and feelings.

START FROM GROUND-UP: BUILD HEALTHY FAMILY DYNAMICS

No matter how much help you obtain from outside organizations, friends, your child's school, and therapists, it is difficult to feel grounded and loved unless your home is a haven for every single family member at the end of the day. Don't be so determined to help your children achieve external goals that the quality of your family relationships suffers. Investing in a happy family environment will help your child with autism in various important ways.

- It will help your child feel more secure, so they can feel more confident about trying new things and meeting new people.
- It will make resolving conflicts that occur in the home easier.
- It will teach all of your children what a healthy and happy family looks and feels like.
- It will teach everyone in your family about the importance of setting healthy limits, communicating assertively, not aggressively or passively, and using healthy language when everyday arguments and conflicts arise.

You can strengthen family relationships by doing several things.

- Teach your children how to identify and deal with difficult emotions in a productive manner. Let them know that it is okay to feel angry, frustrated, or disappointed, but this does not mean it is okay to insult others, hit them, or generally step over their boundaries.
- Teach children to use "I" language such as "I feel sad when you don't let me play this game with you" instead of "you" language such as "You always leave me out," "You never listen to me," or "You enjoy seeing me cry." Encourage children to see conflicts as a positive opportunity to really listen to each other, care about each other's feelings, and make necessary changes that will help your family achieve its goals more frequently.
- Celebrate the fun involved in being part of a family. Take part in activities that everyone enjoys. Ditch your computers and hand-held devices for a weekend and take a camping trip or make weekend hobbies such as watching a film together more fun by making popcorn and setting up a make-shift home movie theater.
- Be a positive role model for your children, especially when it comes to resilience. If, when you are out and about, someone is rude to your child or makes mean comments about them, advocate for your child in a polite, composed way that enables

your children to admire you. Try not to lose your composure. When you let anger take control, you have already lost half the battle.

BUILD A STRONG RELATIONSHIP WITH YOUR PARTNER

Parenting a child with autism can lead to tension between partners, as there may be disagreements about aspects such as the appropriate treatments, schooling, and professionals. For some couples, these challenges bring them closer since their first instinct is to lean on each other for support.

Remember that no two people have been through identical experiences, and they may have different ways of processing hurt and disappointment. Not everyone has grown up in a supportive household where communication, love, and support abound. People also have very different ways of dealing with tension. Some seek closeness, others seek distance. Some people are comfortable talking about the things that cause them pain, while others have difficulty bringing up these matters.

It is also important to avoid sugar-coating problems or putting on an unrealistic front. Studies have shown (Nik Adib et al., 2019) that caregivers of autistic children face increased stress and more significant negative caregiving consequences than those with neurotypically developing children. There is no point in putting on a brave face on days when you feel down. You should neither repress your emotions nor feel like you must hide them from your partner.

PARENTING AN AUTISTIC CHILD IS STRESSFUL

If you have other children, you may have found difficulty making decisions such as the ideal school for them or the languages they should study. When you have a child with autism, there are many more decisions to make. Conflict can arise when:

- You view the challenges of autism differently. Some parents can feel overwhelmed, stressed, anxious, or depressed about autism, while others can view their child's challenges as an opportunity to grow and learn. Parents with a growth mindset tend to take the news better, since they know that everyone can change and become excellent at things they once found challenging. These parents find tasks such as finding the best experts, trying out new therapies, and meeting mentors and parents positive and fulfilling.
- Time spent is unbalanced. Some parents may have to work one or two jobs while another may spend most of their day with their child. If so, both parents should ensure they get quality time with their child on a regular basis and even aim to have some alone time that they and their child cherish (Rudy, 2021).
- There is disagreement about treatments. There are many treatments and therapies for children with autism, and as mentioned above, some are seen as more alternative than others. Parents can disagree about the correct path to take in this respect.
- Financial issues arise. We also talked about some of the biggest financial changes that an autism diagnosis can bring, including the possibility of one partner having to leave their job. When discussing finances, it is important to really listen to each other, not push forward your view as if your partner's opinions don't count. Crunch numbers and try out different arrangements if necessary. If you simply cannot afford to give up your job, come to some sort of compromise. You could, for instance, work part-time and rely on family or friends to pitch in a few hours a day.

You should also research different national and regional organizations that provide grants for families living with autism. These include Autism Cares Today. This organization provides grants of between $1,000 and $5,000 to couples earning under a certain amount. United Healthcare Children's Foundation also grants various amounts if your health insurance does not adequately cover your child's medical needs. The National Autism Association Helping Hand Program awards grants up to $1,500 to families in dire financial need. The Asperger/Autism Network of New England grants up to $500 to families earning below a specific income threshold. Joey's Fund Family Grant Program grants up to $3,000 to families in need of financial assistance. New grants arise every year, so keep calling, checking, and talking to other parents to discover any grants that may be applicable to you.

TAKE CONFLICT SERIOUSLY

Making your way through the challenges posed by autism can be difficult when communication styles, expectations, and decisions vary greatly. If you find that this is the case for you and your partner, couples therapy can be enlightening in terms of helping you listen to your partner, understand them, and come to agreements about important matters after open, honest discussions about various matters.

RELY ON YOUR EXTENDED FAMILY

If you are a perfectionist who likes to take charge of all things you see as your responsibility, try reframing your outlook, at least in respect to caring for your child. If you have an extended family that is eager to play an important role in your children's upbringing and they have the time and energy to do so, consider their interest as highly beneficial to your child.

If someone can bring your child to a therapy appointment once a week, that's one gym workout you could get done, a lunch date you could make, or a personal medical checkup you could have. There is no point in neglecting your own health and happiness because you feel like you must be the perfect parent 24/7.

Different family members can also bring out different talents, abilities, and interests in your child. A family member who is an art aficionado, for instance, may enjoy taking your child to galleries and museums or teaching them how to sketch their favorite subjects. A sporty family friend may be able to teach your child the ins and outs of skating or acrobatics. By introducing your child to a wider social circle, you are expanding their horizons and increasing the likelihood that they will find hobbies and interests that fulfill and de-stress them, or that boost their health, fitness, and quality of life.

ACKNOWLEDGE YOUR CHILD'S CONTRIBUTIONS TO THE FAMILY

Avoid creating a family dynamic in which your child with autism is viewed as a challenge or a problem. Acknowledge the good things they bring to your family and express your thanks verbally so that their siblings are encouraged to be grateful. You might notice, for instance, that your routines run like a well-oiled machine thanks to your child. You may be thankful that you are now closer to extended family than you used to be, or you may notice that your other children are learning qualities like responsibility, empathy, and caring for their sibling with autism. When acknowledging your child's efforts, keep the following in mind:

- Be near them and face them so they know your full attention is on them.
- Use eye contact and body language, such as nodding or smiling, to show you are listening to them.
- Praise specific actions. For instance, you might say, "I noticed you played Sarah's favorite song when she was stressed earlier. Thank you. That was very thoughtful."
- Take a photo of the precious moment if you can.
- Provide your child with the time, opportunities, and materials they need to make their chosen contributions to their home and family.

Ensure that you all see your family as a team, one that may have a few hurdles to jump along the way but that also rises to the occasion by working together (Penn State Extension, n.d.). When someone makes a mistake or fails, be thankful, for failure provides everyone, adults and children alike, with a unique opportunity to grow.

BUILD A SUPPORTIVE TEAM

We mentioned the importance of building team spirit within your family. However, you are also part of a larger support team that involves doctors, therapists, teachers, mentors, caretakers, and anyone else who plays an important role in your child's life. Always remember that even though you are dealing with learned, experienced professionals, the parents are the team leaders, since it is up to them to make the many important decisions. When it comes to mentors, be open to anyone who can help you feel positive and goal-focused, even if they aren't experts in autism. You may enjoy sharing your doubts, worries, and joys with your pastor or with an older family member who always makes you feel a little more inspired after spending time with them.

Your Child's Team of Doctors and Therapists

You may wish to consult various doctors to deal with your child's needs. Just a few specialists you may be directed to include:

- **Child neurologists:** Child neurologists specialize in identifying and treating nervous system and brain disorders. You may decide to consult a child neurologist if your child has significant motor, speech, or language delays. They may also be helpful if your child has low muscle tone or if you are concerned about their social or play skills. You may notice that your child has lost skills they had already previously acquired or that they are showing signs of seizure-like behavior (Interactive Autism Network, 2016). Seizures are slightly more common in children who have autism than in neurotypical kids. Autistic children have a 10% to 20% chance of having a seizure, compared to 1% to 5% in the general population. This specialist may also be able to help if your child has sleeping and feeding issues

- **Pediatric gastroenterologists:** Gastrointestinal (GI) problems can be painful and debilitating, and they can have a profound effect on your child's behavior. GI issues are four times more common in autistic children than in the general population, yet they are often very difficult to detect. Children with autism may not be verbal, and they may have sensory processing impairments that make it impossible for them to pinpoint the cause of their pain or discomfort. GI specialists use special questionnaires and testing methods that have a very high degree of success for diagnoses of GI disorders. Signs that may indicate your child has GI issues include constipation, gagging during meals, applying pressure to the tummy, and arching the back (Columbia University Irving Medical Center, 2018).
- **Specialized pediatricians:** Some board-accredited pediatricians are also trained in developmental-behavioral pediatrics. They speak to parents to obtain detailed information about their child's habits, challenges, and skills and will make useful recommendations for treatment. They can also refer you to specific agencies that fund or provide the therapies and educational programs that can benefit your child.
- **Speech therapists:** Speech therapy is centered on helping your child improve their verbal, nonverbal, and social communication. Therapists help your child acquire useful skills such as strengthening muscles in the neck, jaw, and mouth. They also work with your child on making clearer speech sounds, matching their emotions to the appropriate facial expression, understanding body language, and more.
- **Occupational therapists:** This therapist can help your child with skills like getting dressed independently, eating, and hygiene-related tasks. They also work to improve your child's fine motor skills, the kind they need to use scissors, write, or color a picture.

- **Biomedical experts:** These specialists focus on eliminating problems caused by digestion and nutrient absorption, food sensitivities, impaired detoxification and immune function, and mitochondrial disorders. These specialists sometimes recommend supplements like Omega-3 fatty acids, which are thought to reduce hyperactivity in autistic children, or melatonin to promote better sleep.

Get Teachers Onboard

Get close to your child's teacher so that you can share the strategies that work with your child. As you build trust and friendship with your child's teacher, you can suggest tips such as helping reduce sensory overload. For instance, the teacher might take down distracting posters or use calming colors in class instead of bright ones, or they may avoid playing loud music if this causes distress to your child. Your child's teacher may find that using visuals and encouraging your child to use fidget devices can help them stay calm and focused (Elemy, 2021).

Encourage open communication with the teacher and let them feel free to vent if they've had a hard day. Allow them to be completely honest about your child. By keeping a sense of humor, being empathetic to each other's situations, and taking a solutions-based approach to problems that arise, you and your child's teacher can form a solid and powerful relationship that is honest, positive, and open to trying out new things.

KEY SOURCES OF SUPPORT

In addition to working alongside experienced professionals, you will also find crucial support from other individuals and groups. These can include:

- **The autism community:** There are many ways to be a part of the autism community. One good place to start is The Autism Society, which encourages its members to advocate about autism-related issues, stay abreast of the latest news through its online newsletter, *Autism Matters,* and attend workshops, conferences, and other events in their respective areas. This association has affiliates in many cities and towns. To find an affiliate in your area, call the number 800-3-AUTISM (800-328-8476). The association additionally has a conference page where you can learn about meetings you may like to attend. Another interesting service offered by this group is the free course, Autism 101, which covers everything from treatment options to treatment assistance.

- **Specialists in family therapy, marital or individual counseling:** Health professionals often advise anyone who is experiencing the symptoms of depression or anxiety to see a psychotherapist. Moreover, couples who are having difficulty adjusting to life as parents of an autistic child are often directed to attend marital counseling.

Therapy should not be seen as a last resort. Therapy can help families adjust, adopt healthy patterns of communication, and resolve conflicts positively. Receiving a diagnosis for autism and other conditions that cause big changes in family dynamics may require more than just reading and maintaining a growth mindset.

Family therapy for autism is based on the idea that every family member faces challenges during different stages of a child's life. At the outset, family members can feel confused or shocked. During the toddler years, they may be heavily focused on finding appropriate treatments. As children grow into teens, parents and siblings may worry about the child making friends and being accepted by their peers. When children become adults, parents can turn their focus toward college, jobs, finances, and, if required, caring for their adult children.

Family stress can make life more difficult for a child with autism. Family members who are depressed, anxious, or stressed may be less able to access the best treatment for the person with autism. As a result, a child with autism may act out more, and a harmful cycle may emerge (Children and Family Mental Health, 2009). Family therapy can help all families adopt healthy patterns that will bring out the best in each family member.

ASD Support Groups

There are many support groups for children with autism and their families across the country, and they are considered vital for the children themselves as well as their parents, siblings, family, and friends. Indeed, they can help anyone who needs support or seeks access to more resources (Elemy, 2021). If you wish, you can start by contacting government organizations such as the CDC, the Office of Special Education and Rehabilitative Services Blog, or the Behavioral Health Services Locator.

You can also approach non-profit and community organizations such as Autism Speaks and the Center for Parent Information and Resources. You will also find various state groups by conducting a quick search.

Meet Other Parents and Read Blogs

Local support groups will provide you with plenty of opportunity to meet and greet other parents and share your experiences and information. You can learn more about other parents' perspectives on online forums and blogs. Just a few blogs you may enjoy reading include *Rainbows are Too Beautiful*, *Sensory Spectrum*, *Stages Learning*, *The Autism Dad*, and *The AWEnesty of Autism*.

Rely on Respite Care

Respite care is short-term care that can provide primary caregivers with a little time away from their care duties. Respite care can take many forms, including in-home care, structured care programs, camp programs, and similar programs. To find respite providers and programs in your state, start with the ARCH National Respite Network, which lists resources for finding respite care in specific communities. You can also contact Easterseals, a nationwide organization offering respite care services, camps, and more, and Autism Speaks, which lists over 100 respite care programs.

Respite care can also be provided informally or in a structured manner by family members or close friends. When asking them for help, be specific about the areas in which you need help. Sometimes, loved ones do not offer help because they are afraid they might be overstepping boundaries. If you want their help, let them know.

CHAPTER SUMMARY

Don't try to take on more work or pressure than you can handle. By asking for help when you need it, you can feel more energetic and motivated to be a staunch advocate for your child. Check yourself frequently to ensure you are not overworking, and make sure to:

- Work to build healthy family dynamics.
- Make sure your partner feels loved and cared for.
- Rely on support groups, non-profit organizations, parent groups, and family.
- Build a supportive team comprising various professionals and get teachers onboard, too.
- Meet other parents and share your hopes, fears, and achievements with them.
- Aim to have time off, even if this means finding professional respite care.

Your Unique Opportunity to Be Part
of Another Family's Supportive Team

Be strong, be fearless, be beautiful. And believe that anything is possible when you have the right people there to support you.

MISTY COPELAND

We've discussed the importance of a support network when you're parenting a child with autism, and you already know better than most people how difficult and isolating this journey can be at times.

It can be daunting to look for the support you need when you're used to struggling alone, and the main goal of this book is to help parents like you find their way through. Simply by reading it and finding out more about the strategies you can use to help you cope and help your child thrive, you've become part of a community of parents all working towards the same goal.

Now you have an opportunity to help other parents who are a little farther behind you on the path. Think about how you choose any book or service to help your child—or any activity you're considering signing them up for. The chances are, you read reviews—you want to know how other parents found the product or experience before you commit to it. You want to know whether it's the right thing for you and your child.

By leaving a review of this book on Amazon, you can help other parents who are navigating the same path find the right guidance for them—you can be part of their support network without ever meeting them.

When you leave your honest opinion of this book on Amazon and describe how it's helped you, other parents will be able to gauge whether it's the resource they're looking for. Without the effort of more than a couple of minutes, you will have become part of another parent's support network.

I can't thank you enough for your help with this. No parent is an island, and without your support, I wouldn't be able to connect with half of the people who are seeking support.

Scan this QR code for the review link

CHAPTER 6
PREPARE FOR YOUR CHILD'S FUTURE FINANCIAL INDEPENDENCE

I t is a tough question, but it is one that nearly all parents may ask themselves at one point or another: "What will happen to my child when I am no longer around?" Of course, life can be unpredictable, but in general, we know that our children will most likely outlive us. The thought that they might not have adequate shelter, food, love, or care is devastating. From the outset, it is important to take the necessary steps to ensure their needs will be met when they are older.

"The diagnosis was just a confirmation of what I already knew. I didn't cry, I was just concerned about what the future would look like." — *Suzanne Kohler*

FINANCIAL PLANNING FOR TWO GENERATIONS

Parents of a child with special needs may have to plan for their own lifetime care as well as that of their child. Such is the case if your child is not in a position to make financial decisions when they are older or if they require various types of care. The aim is to maintain your child's current standard of living when you are no longer around (Chakraborty, 2018).

Research indicates that young adults with autism are more likely to live with their parents after leaving high school compared to those with other types of disabilities. To be precise, while some 21% of all young adults in the US lived at home with a parent in their early 20s, around 87% of people with autism lived with a parent at some point after leaving high school. Moreover, around five times as many young adults with autism lived with a parent or guardian in their early 20s compared to those who lived independently or in supervised living arrangements (Drexel University, 2015). Few lived in supervised settings, on their own, with a partner, or roommates.

PLAN FOR YOUR CHILD'S LIVING ARRANGEMENTS

Your financial situation, along with your child's wishes and independence levels, will determine which of the many possible living options is best (Price, 2021). For your child, the list of options may include:

- **Living with you at home:** If you are a homeowner, you can leave your home to your child in a special needs trust. You can make accommodations to your home that will enable your child to live more independently. You could construct a self-contained living area on the grounds of your home. This home can be detached or part of your dwelling, and it essentially functions as a miniature home that comes with amenities such as a kitchen.
- **Buying a separate home for your child:** This property can also form part of a special needs trust. Medicaid and Supplemental Security Income regulations allow beneficiaries to own a home without losing their eligibility for benefits.
- **Living in a supported home or apartment:** In this model, adults with autism can live alone or as tenants or owner-occupiers, and they can continue to receive supported living services.
- **Group homes:** Some parents pool their funds together to provide group homes for their children. An adult with autism

can also use their Medicaid payments or private funds for this purpose. Within a group home setting, care is sometimes provided by caregivers or counselors.

- **Section 8 vouchers**: These belong to a federal program for low-income earners. It entitles them to live in community housing. Unfortunately, waiting lists can be long.
- **Government assistance:** Your child may be entitled to government benefits related to housing. For instance, the Section 811 Housing Program provides help with rent for persons with disabilities who are earning a low income. The Interagency Autism Coordinating Committee offers a thorough online directory that lists government and private organizations that offer information or provide help with housing options (Interagency Autism Coordinating Committee, n.d.).

When choosing one of the above options, you should also consider family sources. Your child may have siblings, other relatives, or close family friends who can provide support for your child, or they may wish to set up a self-contained living area in their home. Your choice will ultimately depend on a combination of three factors: existing family support, costs, and the amount of daily support your child requires.

Factors Linked to the Living Arrangements of People With Autism

Key factors that are linked to living arrangements include:

- **Household incomes:** Almost 40% of young adults with autism who come from upper income households lived independently at some point, compared to only 6% of those from lowest income households.
- **Race and ethnicity:** Most young adults who lived independently were white, rather than black or Hispanic.

- **Conversation skills:** Almost 45% of young adults with the highest level of conversation skills lived independently, compared to none of those with the lowest skill level.

Housing

As mentioned above, government housing assistance for people with autism is limited. Medicaid cuts are only making matters worse, since many people with disabilities rely on Medicaid to pay for their housing. As pointed out by Autism Spectrum News' Mandy H. Breslow (2019), the average rent for a one-bedroom apartment is approximately 104% of the average SSI benefit. This is a worry for many adults with disabilities who may not be able to rent a place of their own. While there are programs that are addressing this issue across the nation, many are full. Enabling adults with autism to live independently is wise from a financial perspective, since the average cost to place and care for people in a group home can cost up to $140,000 a year. By encouraging people to live independently and providing them with support, tens of thousands of dollars per person could be saved every year.

In addition to these considerations, you should also add up any expenses for safety, vocational services, home care, and any other current or future expenses your child may have.

AUTISM AND EMPLOYMENT

Although statistics are scarce, the available data indicates that only around one-third of adults with autism work in paid jobs for more than 15 hours per week. This mirrors results in the UK, where around 22% are in any kind of employment. As pointed out by Politico's Michael Bernick (2021), many positive strides have been made in supporting people with autism, especially in the areas of education, housing, and mental health programs. However, the area of employment is still lagging.

Bernick argues that for people with autism to secure stable employment, they must find positions where they can add value and be able to access workplaces that truly recognize what they have to offer. A truly autism-friendly workplace, then, is not one that simply boasts physical elements that can make work easier for employees with autism. It must also value patience and flexibility and give new employees the time they need to master new skills, both work- and behavior-related.

To make a real difference, governments need to invest in the intensive employment services system. Staff should not have such a heavy workload that they do not have enough time to really match each worker with the right organization and role. Currently, a handful of entities, both nonprofit and for-profit, are helping to bridge the gap for people with autism. They include Autism Speaks Employment, EVOLVE, Zavikon, Uptimize, Integrate, NeuroTalent Works, Potentia, Evolibri, and SourceAbled. Their work is focused on helping people with autism enter the private sector.

QUESTIONS TO ASK YOURSELF

When planning out finances for your child, it is important to ascertain the extent to which your child needs assistance. If your child can manage to get and keep employment, you may not need to plan for their entire lifetime. Whatever the case may be, it is important to start planning early, as soon as your child receives their diagnosis.

Once you know the amount of financial planning required, set goals, save, and invest accordingly. Set short- and long-term goals. Obtain help from a financial planner, if possible, as they can suggest ways to grow your funds over time. For short-term goals, debt funds or fixed deposits may be ideal, while equity mutual funds may be useful for long-term goals. It all depends on the nature of your assets and the types of investments you are most comfortable with.

Don't make any financial decisions lightly. Speak to mentors, investors, and advisors to ensure your plans are neither too conservative nor too risky (Mehta, 2021). Make sure that your own retirement is covered in your plans, and choose the one that will give you the best tax advantages.

You should also consider taking out a whole life insurance policy, which will remain active so long as the premiums are paid. That way, your child will receive the death benefit no matter when you pass away. The premiums on this type of policy are higher, but they build up a cash value you can access prior to death if needed (Van Keuren, 2021). If your child is receiving governmental assistance such as Medicaid or Supplemental Security Income, avoid making them the direct beneficiary of a life insurance policy since they could lose their right to assistance. Instead, set up a special needs trust (Brady Cobin Law Group, PLLC, 2021). We will discuss special needs trusts later in this chapter.

FIND A GUARDIAN

Your child may need a guardian on two occasions (Platt, 2022):

- **While you, their parents, are alive**: In this scenario, you would appoint yourself as a guardian, so you can make legal decisions for your child when they turn 18. If you do not become your child's guardian, then they will be responsible for all decisions pertaining to finances, schooling, healthcare, signing contracts, obtaining a credit card or loan, and similar responsibilities. If your child needs help with these areas, then you can start the process of obtaining guardianship around six months before they turn 18.
- **After your death:** During their lifetime, you may select a guardian to care for your child after your death. This person will be able to make decisions about your child's healthcare, expenses, accommodation, and similar areas. In general, you

should only appoint a guardian if there are no less restrictive alternatives. If your child has the capacity to make decisions with respect to aspects such as their IEP, housing and similar, then they will not need a guardian.

Guardianship does not have to be permanent. This means that you may think it appropriate to be your child's guardian until they reach a certain age.

Types of Guardianship

There are various types of guardianship, including:

- **General guardianship:** In this case, the guardian cares for the person's estate and their daily decisions. In general, unless the person with a disability has an estate, they don't need such an all-encompassing guardianship. Usually, they will not have assets in their own name, so they can qualify for benefits and grants. A general guardianship allows the guardian to make numerous decisions about various aspects, including:
- end-of-life care decisions
- moving home or location
- making all healthcare decisions, including those pertaining to medications, treatment, and surgery
- estate management, including the payment of bills and purchases
- **Limited guardianship:** This type of guardianship grants the guardian the power to make only those decisions about personal care and finances that the court specifies. With this, you can specify areas in which your child will continue to have autonomy.

When making your selection, consider a limited guardianship so that your child can continue to enjoy as much independence as possible. It can be more difficult to limit the extent of your control, but it may benefit and empower them in important ways.

ESTATE AND FINANCIAL PLANNING FOR YOUR CHILD

When you have children, their future will be something you worry about from the time they are born. Parents usually aim to set aside funds for college and other expenses. When it comes to a child with autism, financial planning is even more important, since you must ensure that your child is well taken care of and that your absence does not mean they may lack adequate food, clothing, accommodations, treatments, medication, and all the other things they need to be healthy and happy.

Even if you are financially well-off, simply leaving money to your child will not ensure they are properly cared for when you're gone. Moreover, doing so can put their state or federal benefits at risk. Leaving matters to the goodwill of others without formal planning could put your child in a very vulnerable position. Having a formal, watertight plan of action means that every possible contingency will be taken care of.

Planning for your child's future can be tricky. Nobody enjoys contemplating their own mortality and its effect on their family. Estate planning requires you to crunch numbers, anticipate expenses, and make challenging decisions, but once you get this important task out of the way, you will definitely enjoy a better night's sleep knowing no stone has been left unturned.

Important Issues to Consider

Before starting the process of estate planning, think about the following issues:

Education

Is your child interested in pursuing further education, or are they already enrolled in a college or other tertiary institution? The average cost of tuition and fees to attend a private college in the US stands at around $38,185 a year, while an in-state, public college costs around $10,388 a year to attend. A public, out-of-state college, meanwhile, will set you back approximately $22,698 a year (Powell et al., 2021).

Medical Costs

In Chapter Three, it was mentioned that while most health-related costs are covered by insurance, families still pay approximately $4,000 more in out-of-pocket expenses than families without children who have autism. Your child's medical costs could potentially be higher, of course, if they are currently undergoing alternative or additional therapies.

Last Will and Testament

Your will should stipulate aspects such as the distribution of your estate, and it should include the name of your child's future guardian. You may also consider making a living will, which stipulates what actions should be taken for your health if, for any reason, you are unable to make decisions for yourself because of illness or incapacity.

Letter of Intent

You should also consider drafting a letter of intent, which is not a legal document per se, but it does provide guardians, trustees, and service providers with important information regarding your child's needs, preferences, and habits, as well as their family history (Autism Society, n.d.). This letter can include information such as:

- Your family history and memories relating to yourself and other family members and your child
- Medical history, medications, and health professionals treating your child
- Benefits your child is currently receiving
- Dietary requirements or preferences
- Behavior strategies that work well with your child
- Current educational programs and future plans
- Activities and hobbies your child enjoys
- Career-related interests

- End-of-life preferences

When writing your letter of intent, try to include your child in the process to ensure you haven't left out any important details or wishes.

Durable Power of Attorney

A durable power of attorney enables a person to act on behalf of another if they become incapacitated. You will need to grant this power to someone so they can take over your role as power of attorney.

Financial Representative

It is reassuring to know that there is now a specialization in law that deals with helping people with autism obtain financial security. In 2018, financial planner Andrew Komarow, who was diagnosed with autism at the age of 27, founded Planning Across the Spectrum (Rusoff, 2020). This organization helps guide parents of autistic children through a maze of support services, government disability benefits, and financial plans. It is always a good idea to have a financial representative who specializes in this niche on your side.

Setting Up a Special Needs Trust

A special needs trust aims to provide your child with the individualized care they need while protecting their eligibility for public benefits. In order to set one up, you will need to hire an experienced attorney who specializes in this field. You will then need to choose a trustee to take charge of trust management and administration. You will also need to complete your letter of intent.

The funds for your special needs trust can come from existing assets, such as life insurance, which will provide your children with an income-free and estate tax-free death benefit, and your estate. The special needs trust, instead of your child, should be stipulated as the beneficiary in your will.

Regardless of the plan you choose, you should reassess it every five to ten years, as your child's needs, circumstances, or wishes may change over time.

There are different types of special needs trusts:

- **A first-party trust**: This is usually established for assets that would otherwise go straight to your child. It is ideal if the beneficiary is to receive significant assets because there are no restrictions on how it can be used. However, when the beneficiary dies, the remaining money is first used to pay the state for medical aid provided by a state Medicaid plan (Brady Cobin Law Group, PLLC, 2021).
- **A third-party special needs trust:** This type of trust can hold any type of asset that is not owned by the beneficiary, including investment portfolios, life insurance policies, or properties that produce income.
- **A pooled special needs trust:** This trust is managed by a non-profit organization instead of a single trustee. It allows a disabled person to retain unlimited assets without being disqualified from government assistance. Under this arrangement, once you turn over your money, you cannot control how it is invested or spent. Moreover, the manager chosen by the non-profit organization, rather than a family member or friend, oversees the trust. When the beneficiary dies, the trust typically keeps some of the account to help fund other pooled trusts.

EMPOWER YOUR CHILD TO LIVE MORE INDEPENDENTLY

Encourage your child to be independent, motivated, and daring. Inspire them to see the value of experiencing life to the fullest and to have a growth mindset. As much as you love your child, you may not always be around for them, and the more skills they pick up, the better off they will be in the long run. Tips for boosting their independent spirit include:

- Help them find work opportunities. This includes unpaid work experience and paid part- or full-time work.
- Encourage them to volunteer. Help them find something they are passionate about, be it animals, the elderly, or the environment. Find out what's going on in your community and go along with your child or encourage them to attend events like beach or city clean-ups.
- Find social opportunities for your child. These can range from free outdoor yoga in the park to group gym classes like spin or dance classes. When choosing from different options, build on your child's strengths and interests.
- Make sure your child is signed up for Social Security Disability Income (SSDI). This provides monthly benefits to people who have a disability that restricts their ability to be employed.
- Remember that all men aged between 18 and 25 must register with Selective Service, the "draft." Even though your son is registered, it does not mean they will automatically be inducted into the military.
- Make sure your child is registered to vote. Because the amount of information sent out prior to elections can be overwhelming, the Autistic Self Advocacy Network has created a handy guide called Your Vote Counts. It explains aspects such as what voting is, why it is important to vote, the difference between a primary and general election, and more. The guide is available in easy read and plain language versions (Autistic Self Advocacy Network, n.d.).

When planning for your child's future, it is critically important to include them in the process and to have open, honest conversations. Keeping records updated and handy is also important. If anything happens to you, your other children or other loved ones should know exactly where to find key documentation.

CHAPTER SUMMARY

Planning for your child's future is vital for your peace of mind. Steps you should take to leave important financial matters in order include the following:

- Finding a trusted guardian for your child
- Writing your last will and testament
- Involving your child in writing a thorough letter of intent
- Granting a durable power of attorney
- Seeking the help of a financial representative to make the best possible choices for your child
- Setting up a special needs trust
- Encouraging your child to form a supportive social network
- Empowering your child to enjoy the ups and downs of the quest for independence

CHAPTER 7
MISTAKES TO AVOID

P arents can mean well and make great efforts to ensure their children are healthy and happy. However, if you have more than one child, then you know that each one takes time to work out and adapt to. Everyone makes mistakes, and in the early stages, a lack of information, experience, and/or resources, or a desire to protect your child to the greatest extent possible, can lead you to commit unintended mistakes.

Try to see mistakes as your greatest teacher. Do not judge yourself if you have an off-day and remember that you are so much more than your mistakes. Every new day is a chance to refine your strategies or avoid thoughts, beliefs, and words that can interfere with the achievement of your goals.

HIDING YOUR CHILD'S DIAGNOSIS

If you hide your child's diagnosis from your wider circle, you will be taking on a burden and a level of stress that you don't need (Prasad, 2017). It will also send an unspoken message to your child that they are not good enough to be accepted as they are. Lies and half-truths are uncomfortable and sometimes impossible to sustain. They impose pressure on yourself and anyone else in your family who must hide information that they would normally reveal.

Sharing your child's diagnosis gets rid of many problems at once. It enables others to understand your child, and it reduces the likelihood of judgment and criticism. The truth frees you of the need to make excuses and sugarcoat reality. It allows you to tell others when you must leave because you have to take your child to an appointment or because you are attending an IEP meeting. Being open enables others to get closer to you and your child.

By confiding in others, you are showing them that you trust them. This can also bring you many surprises. For instance, you may tell a friend about your child and discover that they grew up with a sibling with autism. This powerful discovery can create an unbreakable bond and strengthen your friendship. It can also result in learning and growth. Everyone has information and experiences to share, and these may be useful to you in your own decision-making process. Autism is not something to be ashamed of or afraid of. It affects millions of people across the globe, and it simply requires different approaches and therapies.

ASSUMING CHALLENGING BEHAVIOR IS A TANTRUM

If you are out one day and your child starts to display challenging behavior, do not assume that it is a tantrum or that your child is trying to be difficult. It is easy to feel frustrated, especially if you have had a hard day or are stressed. However, to the greatest extent possible, you should aim to take a few deep breaths and analyze what was occurring in the moments before your child began acting out.

Your careful reflection will reveal that there is a select list of reasons that may account for what occurred. It can include anxiety, sensory issues, and a lack of coping skills. If you assume it is just your child trying to annoy you, you could be missing something like anxiety, which needs to be dealt with as an independent condition. Making assumptions also stops you from making important discoveries.

As hard as it is, you need to take a step back and try to be a fly on the wall or see what is occurring from a more distant, objective perspective. Did you do anything different today that may have made them uncomfortable? Were there any loud sounds, colors, or lights that may have overburdened their senses? Did someone say something unkind or take their comfort toy from their hands? Did they have a restless night, and could they just be tired? The information you compile will enable you to reduce the prevalence or severity of unpleasant situations for your child. It will also enable you to feel more confident about the way you structure your child's day. Be wary of signs of other issues such as anxiety. If your child seems to be having a panic attack, speak to your medical team about it. Anxiety requires specific approaches. Many may actually overlap with those you are already using, including controlled breathing and meditation.

THINKING YOUR CHILD ISN'T SMART

All children have academic strengths and weaknesses. Just because a child may struggle more in one or more subjects does not mean they cannot learn and thrive in others. Observe your child with honesty and openness. Help them in areas where they are struggling and celebrate those they are passionate about. Share your experiences with good friends and parents who you know have your child's best interests at heart. They will most probably share their own struggles with you. For instance, they may have a child who is a whiz at math but who struggles at physical education.

Avoid engaging in conversations that are centered on competitiveness. Talk at the school gates can be detrimental to your well-being. Steer clear of those whose conversation involves talking about other children or comparing or complaining about other children's behavior.

THINKING AUTISM IS THE SAME THING AS SOCIAL AVERSION

If a child does not engage in eye contact, people can mistakenly assume that it means they are indifferent to other people, a situation, an experience, or a social interaction. Research has shown that toddlers with autism who avoid eye contact do so because they can be oblivious to the social information contained in another person's eyes (Tsang, 2018). A toddler with autism may indeed show indifference to social stimuli, including faces and people, and miss out on social learning opportunities. When they grow older, they can then continue this behavior simply because they do not feel a need to look into another person's eyes.

However, avoiding eye contact does not mean that a child is avoiding social interaction or that they are uncomfortable when looking into someone else's eyes. On the contrary, research on school-aged children with autism indicates that they have a deep desire to create meaningful friendships with other children, but they may struggle with the skills that are required to achieve this goal. The good news is that social skills training can help. This type of training introduces a reward system to teach children how to recognize verbal and non-verbal subtleties of communication and apply useful social skills. During social skills training, therapists may use pictures of faces, group practice, and videos or software to teach children about body language and communication (Otsimo, 2018).

EXPECTING OTHERS TO BE KNOWLEDGEABLE ABOUT AUTISM

People you encounter casually and even close friends and family can sometimes say the wrong thing because they lack knowledge about autism. Trust your instincts. If you feel that someone has made an honest mistake and you have the time and inclination to do so, you can share vital information with them. When you are explaining autism, start with the basics and explain how it affects your child specifically (Carmen B. Pingree Autism Center of Learning, n.d.). For instance, you might explain that your child finds it very challenging when you veer from their routine or that they avoid making eye contact.

Feel free to mention positive traits your child has as well. These may include an ability to focus deeply on a subject, pay attention to detail, or remember an array of interesting facts about a topic they are interested in.

Try to see this conversation as a way to remove the person's confusion about how to interact with your child. For instance, if you are in their home visiting, you can let them know about any sensory or food sensitivities your child may have. Let them know about the current goals you are working on. You may be working on getting your child used to a new activity, or you may be helping them master the art of reading facial expressions and body language via social skills training.

COMPARING YOUR CHILD TO OTHERS

Parents of toddlers and young children often make the mistake of comparing their children to others. Doing so is natural because you wonder if your child is doing okay, especially if you don't have other children. However, comparison can be harmful for both you and your child. Try to avoid getting into conversations that are heavily focused on phrases like "Is your child walking/reading/talking/adding up numbers already?" "What reading level is your child on?" Parents can also sometimes compare behaviors or proudly state that their children are "doing right." It is not uncommon to hear sentences like "Your child is so nervous/restless/chatty. My Anna is the opposite. She is relaxed and so well behaved."

Some parents can become incredibly competitive and constantly seek to measure their child's achievements or behavior against yours. Invest your time in empathetic, kind people, and check yourself if you find yourself having these thoughts. Many parents have experienced that as their child got older, things like reading levels and math skills leveled out, and the futility of comparing and competing became clearer than ever.

Celebrate your child's uniqueness, as this is what sets them apart. Their hobbies, interests, and talents could lead to an interesting career choice in the future, or they could lead to interesting conversations. Do not be ashamed to talk about your child's strengths to teachers, therapists, doctors, and friends (DiProperzio, 2021). When you talk about your child to other parents, though, make sure that no comparison with their children is involved. Rely on your instinct to lead you to good people who will cherish your child's achievements and never feel the need to put them down.

FORCING INTERESTS ONTO YOUR CHILD

All parents can be a little guilty of sometimes forcing their own interests, or those they deem important, onto their children. For example, you may have loved baseball as a child and be eager for your child to get into the sport. Amanda was a big sports enthusiast who was always cycling or training for a marathon in her spare time. When her daughter Arris was born, she planned on passing on her love for health and fitness to her. However, Arris was more interested in all things having to do with marine life. When she was not watching videos about her favorite species, she was drawing or reading about them, and she liked nothing more than visiting the aquarium.

It can be a little disappointing when a child does not share your personal passions. However, if you look back at your own life, you will probably see that many of your interests were picked up along your life's journey. Not all of them were experienced for the first time through your parents or siblings.

As your child grows up and matures, you will surely develop a few overlapping interests, whether it's reading, watching films, or gourmet dining, and you will be able to bond over these subjects and activities.

REFUSING TO ASK FOR HELP

In his popular blog, *Autistic & Unapologetic*, James Ward-Sinclair (2017) states an important truth: "One of the most powerful words in the English language is 'help'." By simply using that word, difficult and rocky paths can become much smoother. There are many reasons, however, why "help" can be such a difficult word to say, including pride, a fear of bothering others, taking up too much of someone's time, and a fear of being perceived as vulnerable.

By taking on increasingly heavier burdens and more tasks than you can reasonably handle, you are increasing your likelihood of stress, depression, anxiety, and burnout. Any parent of a child with autism may need help with tasks such as caring for their child so they can have some-time off or attend to important tasks. When you ask for help and receive it, you enable yourself and your child to attain important goals. You also strengthen your bond with others by showing that you trust them enough to let them into your life and help you with things that matter to you. Asking for help is part and parcel of the human condition. In the words of motivational speaker Les Brown, "Ask for help. Not because you are weak, but because you want to remain strong."

DRAWING UNWARRANTED CONCLUSIONS

Being the parent of a child with autism requires you to bring your best detective skills to the forefront. Especially in your child's early years, you will be observing things like their triggers and biggest sources of comfort and making lists of everything from the foods they dislike to situations that stress them out. However, sometimes things occur by coincidence. Drawing conclusions as to what caused a specific event can sometimes be helpful, but you should have evidence before doing so. When in doubt, run your thoughts by your child's medical team. They have access to a wider body of both scientific and anecdotal information, and they can help you consider other causes that could have led to a specific behavior or reaction.

Making Belief-Based, Rather Than Evidence-Based, Decisions

We all have beliefs about the world, many of which we learn when we are children ourselves. However, when it comes to important things like raising your child, the beliefs you hold should be backed by evidence. All human beings are prone to biases that can lead to faulty reasoning (Ray, 2021). Relying on science as a way to come closer to the truth can minimize our chance of making decisions based on bias. It also stops the anchoring effect in its tracks. Anchoring occurs when we attach ourselves to a single idea or piece of evidence and make future decisions based on the original information, even if subsequent evidence refutes it.

In order to stay at the top of your game, make sure to research, stay updated on new findings, approaches, and treatments, and avoid seeing issues as falling into an either/or category. Sometimes, the answer to a dilemma lies within a spectrum and is not a matter of choosing between two options.

Also, make it a point to avoid trying every miracle cure that comes your way. Unfortunately, there are people and companies that try to take advantage and sell parents products or services that are not helpful and may be costly. When it comes to treatments, make sure to run everything by a team with scientific knowledge and experience.

OVERINDULGING YOUR CHILD OR BEING EXCESSIVELY VIGILANT

As a loving parent, you want to ensure that all your child's needs and wants are met. However, there is a clear distinction between indulging and overindulging a child. For instance, if you are outdoors and a fireworks spectacle begins, your child may ask you to leave because the loud bangs and crackles of fireworks may sound like a bomb to them, even though these sounds may seem exciting to you. Leaving such a scene is the right thing to do to avoid sensory overload.

However, this does not mean that you always have to say "yes" to your child. For example, if your child wants to play with an electronic toy when it is time to do homework, you don't have to say "yes." Of course, you don't have to say "no" either, and if you can, avoid doing so. Try using positive phrases such as, "Oh, you want your tablet? Of course, you can play with it after you finish your homework." Below are a few positive phrases that show how to redirect your child's attention to another activity or simply ask them to do something.

- "Show me soft touch with the puppy."
- "Show me good steak cutting."
- "First homework then playtime."

Provide plenty of praise for appropriate new behaviors. This is one of the most important parts of achieving positive change. Be specific when doing so. You might say, "You make me so happy when you pet the puppy softly," "You did a great job of cutting that big steak," or "Wow, you did your homework so well by yourself." You can also reinforce good behavior by providing them with a small piece of their favorite treat, a soft toy they love, their tablet, and similar rewards (Tanasugarn,n.d.).

PUTTING YOURSELF LAST ON THE LIST

In the next and final chapter, we will go into the importance of making time to care for yourself and exercising self-compassion and self-kindness. You are the leader of your child's team, and you cannot make good decisions if you are tired, burned out, or anxious. Make sure to keep your health in check. See the dentist regularly and go for all the check-ups and visits your doctor recommends. Seek mental health support if necessary and embrace a healthy lifestyle comprising good food, regular exercise, and proactive stress relief. Remember that the years can fly by quickly, and your child will only get stronger and more resilient with time. For parents, greater care may need to be given to their health as they approach middle age.

CHAPTER SUMMARY

No parent is perfect, and mistakes are not only a part of life but also priceless learning opportunities. Remember to be kind to yourself, and if you do slip up, remember that your actions do not define you. You can always do it differently the next time you are in a similar situation. When going through daily life with your child, keep the following tips in mind:

- Share your child's diagnosis with people you trust.
- Do not assume your child is having a meltdown because they are out to ruin your day.
- Know that your child has their own strengths and weaknesses. Don't expect them to fit into a set mold or be good at the same things as anyone else. They are unique, and it is okay to struggle with some subjects or activities.
- Do not assume that your child is indifferent to what you are doing or saying. It may seem like they aren't listening to you, but they may be absorbing everything.
- Do not expect others to be autism-aware or to know the correct language to use when talking to you about your child. If they make a mistake, be thankful for the opportunity to share your knowledge and raise their awareness of autism.
- Avoid comparing your child to others. This will only hurt them and you.
- Avoid drawing causal conclusions when the things you are observing could simply be correlations or coincidences.
- Neither overindulge nor coddle your child.
- Avoid miracle cures that do not have scientific evidence.
- Do not put your needs and health last.

CHAPTER 8
CARE FOR THE CAREGIVER

As mentioned in Chapter Seven, parents often put their children's needs first and their own needs last. However, being a parent is hard work, and by taking care of yourself, you can give those you love the very best of you. As your child's strongest advocate and supporter, you need to feel healthy and confident, and you need to be in a good place mentally. This cannot happen unless you see your own health, happiness, and well-being as worthwhile goals. When it comes to parenting, self-care isn't optional; it is essential.

HARNESS THE POWER OF SELF-CARE ROUTINES

Self-care isn't simply about occasionally visiting a spa for a massage or having a long soak in your bath, though it can definitely involve these pampering routines. The routines you choose do not have to be complicated or take up too much time, but they should have key characteristics. They should be proactive, and their effect should be to restore physical, mental, and, if you're so inclined, spiritual balance.

A good self-care routine is something that should make you feel good. There are many tried-and-tested components of popular routines that may not strike a chord with you. For instance, yoga has been proven in study after study to lower levels of the stress hormone cortisol. It has helped countless people recover from illness, enhance their focus, and get into a better frame of mind. However, if the mere thought of doing an asana and struggling to maintain your balance makes you cringe but the thought of an upbeat house music spin class sets your heart on fire, then dump that dreaded yoga class and put on your cycling shorts.

The activities you choose should make you feel on top of the world without harming other areas of your life. Just a few of the more popular self-care routines can include:

- Reciting mantras or positive affirmations to yourself when you wake up in the morning
- Visiting a nature-filled area during your lunch break. You don't need a lot of time for this activity. A recent Cornell University study has shown (Meredith et al., 2020) that as little as 10 minutes in a natural setting can help people feel happier and less physically and mentally stressed.
- Practicing controlled breathing for five minutes while you are driving or commuting to and from work: Apps like Breathe, Calm, and Headspace all have relaxing activities you can listen to on your headphones.
- Preparing a healthy packed lunch for work every day
- Participating in your community
- Getting your hair or nails done regularly
- Meeting your friends at a restaurant for dinner
- Pursuing further study
- Learning to dance
- Learning a new language
- Taking at least one or two quality vacations a year
- Training for a triathlon
- Taking part in a fundraising project
- Visiting friends or family

PRIORITIZE SELF-KINDNESS OVER SELF-CONFIDENCE

Having good self-esteem and self-confidence is important in order to make good decisions, sustain relationships, and have good emotional health and overall wellness. However, it is vital to value self-kindness just as much. A study by Duke University scientists (Science Daily, 2007) found that being good to yourself is a key to weathering life's challenges. It helps you recover from the anger, sadness, and pain we can feel when things don't go our way.

Self-kindness differs vastly from self-confidence. While the latter depends to a great extent on the things we achieve, self-kindness is unconditional. It adds a layer of protection that stops self-recrimination from making life's disappointments worse.

Exercising self-kindness or self-compassion involves three behavioral components:

1. Be good to yourself instead of critical. Treat yourself with the same compassion and understanding you share with your loved ones.
2. Understand that negative experiences are common to all human beings.
3. Accept painful thoughts and feelings mindfully instead of over-identifying with them.

REMEMBER THE POWER OF YOUR THOUGHTS

All human beings have positive and negative thoughts and emotions, and neither should be repressed. In fact, studies have shown that the more people worry about being happy, the sadder they become (Honeybourne, 2021). Instead of trying to be happy, try focusing on boosting your resilience and self-awareness in the following ways:

- Acknowledge the things you have accomplished and try to be grateful for the good things in your life and for the help,

support, and love you receive. Research by George Mason
University researchers showed that one of the key ingredients
for living a good life is gratitude (Science Daily, 2009).

- Celebrate small goals as well as large ones. Break up large
  goals into smaller ones so you can enjoy many celebrations
  along the way.

- Choose your battles. You can't get on every soapbox. While it
  is important to be an advocate for your child and not put up
  with substandard treatment, it is equally vital to be discerning
  with what you should complain about. Nobody wants to be
  considered difficult, irritable, or entitled. Do not shy away
  from asking for something your child needs or inquiring about
  an approach that you feel may not be working for your child.
  However, when speaking to teachers, caregivers, therapists,
  doctors, and anyone who has your child's health and well-
  being in their hands, be respectful. Speak assertively, not
  aggressively. Use confident yet calm body language, maintain
  a sense of humor, and always try to put yourself in the other
  person's shoes.

- Trust your gut instinct as a parent. Making decisions is one of
  the most mysterious facets of being human, and most of us are
  taught as children to weigh our options carefully before taking
  a plunge. We previously spoke of the importance of letting
  evidence rather than belief be our guide. However, you have
  another ally on your side: your instinct. Researchers at Tel Aviv
  University's School of Psychological Sciences conducted a
  study (Tsetsos et al, 2012) which showed that intuition was a
  surprisingly powerful, accurate tool. Even at the intuitive level,
  people consider the positive and negative aspects of each
  option to come up with an overall picture. The researchers
  believe that the brain has a built-in ability to average out the
  value of different options so we can make a sound decision.

ADOPT HEALTHY PRACTICES

There are many healthy, positive activities you can carry out either alone or in the company of your loved ones. As mentioned above, there is no one-size-fits-all solution when it comes to the hobbies and activities that fulfill you and boost your well-being. Just a few healthy practices you and your family might enjoy include the following:

- Have fun family rituals. Movie and popcorn nights, lunch out on Sundays, or a weekly ball game with friends at the park. All these rituals fill up your memory bank and boost feelings of family closeness.
- Get out of the house. It is important to spend time in nature. Sometimes, simply changing your environment does wonders for your body, mind, and spirit.
- Keep a journal. Journaling is a powerful way to lower stress levels. A Michigan State University study (Schroder et al, 2017) found that simply writing about your feelings can help you perform future stressful tasks more efficiently. Journaling enables you to get worries out of your head and onto paper. Once you do, your cognitive resources become more efficient, and you can focus on carrying out important tasks more efficiently.
- Share your thoughts and feelings with a trusted friend or family member. Talking about your thoughts and emotions helps you let out tension. You may find that when you are at your lowest, spending time with a close friend or family member helps you feel better, as does having a good cry. However, talking to others about important matters has an added, practical benefit: it invites collaboration and enables you to solve problems in ways you may not have considered.
- Take up a hobby you always loved. People with hobbies are less likely to suffer from low moods, stress, and depression (Head to Health, n.d.).

- Take part in creative pursuits. Activities such as painting, drawing, sculpting, music, and theater can all help keep stress at bay. The good news is that you don't have to be an expert at the arts to benefit from it. Even absolute beginners can benefit just as much from creativity (University of Victoria, n.d.).

REDUCE STRESS

If you feel stressed, pinpoint the cause of stress so you can address it better. Common reasons why people can feel anxious or stressed out include working too many hours, taking on too many obligations, and failing to delegate duties. Try to eliminate as many sources of unnecessary tension from your life as you can. Understandably, some difficult circumstances cannot be changed. However, you can mitigate their effects on your life by embracing practices that promote calm, renew energy, and result in a more positive mood.

- **The Power of Holistic Practices:** Yoga, mindfulness meditation, and Tai Chi have been shown to reduce stress in people of all age groups. They can be as helpful for children as they are for parents. One pilot study undertaken at Vanderbilt University Medical Center showed that Mindfulness-Based Stress Reduction (MBSR), which can lower stress and promote better sleep, can benefit parents of autistic children. In the study, parents of three-year-old autistic children were randomly assigned to attend either a 12-session parenting education program alone or the same program combined with MBSR sessions. Although both groups enjoyed a reduction in stress, the MBSR group also showed lower parental distress and fewer unhealthy parent-child interactions (Bullock, 2020).
- **The Psychological Benefits of Exercise:** Numerous studies have shown that exercise can boost one's mental health in many ways. It can help with depression and anxiety, boost your self-esteem and self-confidence, promote better sleep,

improve your brain health, and provide you with an activity you look forward to completing regularly. In exercise class, you can meet like-minded people who can form an additional support group. As stated by Casper ter Kuile, a Professor at the Harvard Divinity School, for millennials and other upcoming generations, activities such as CrossFit and SoulCycle provide meaning, community, and ritual to those who practice them (Burton, 2018). He states, "People come (to CrossFit and SoulCycle classes) because they want to lose weight or gain muscle strength, but they stay for the community. It's really the relationships that keep them coming back."

GET A GOOD NIGHT'S SLEEP

Resting well every night can help you feel more energetic and focused, and it can help keep problems like stress and anxiety at bay. Aim to get seven to nine hours of sleep at night, and remember that good sleep is a matter of quality as well as quantity. The Sleep Foundation (2021) describes good sleep quality as:

- Falling asleep within half an hour of getting into bed
- Waking up no more than once during the night
- Falling back asleep within 20 minutes if you do wake up
- Feeling renewed and re-energized when you wake up

Try to go to sleep at the same-time every night, avoid caffeine in the afternoon, avoid using screens as they can keep you alert, and invest in good bedroom design. The place where you sleep should be completely dark, cool, and soundproof.

EAT HEALTHY FOODS

Over the past few years, studies have shown that there is an important link between gut and brain health. For instance, scientists have found

(Colomer et al., 2019) that specific groups of microorganisms are positively or negatively linked to mental health. People with depression tend to have lower levels of two bacteria in their gut, *coprococcus* and *dialister*.

The key to good gut health is to consume a wide array of healthy foods so that healthy microbiota can flourish. A Mediterranean-style diet is ideal because it is high in fiber. When you don't consume enough fiber, some bacteria are unable to produce the short-chain fatty acids that reduce inflammation and stave off disease. To build a healthy gut microbiome, consume the following foods:

- Whole grains, nuts, vegetables, fruits, and beans
- Dark chocolate and other polyphenol-rich foods which provide fuel for health-giving microbes
- Fermented foods like kimchi, kefir, sauerkraut, kombucha, tempeh, natto, and miso
- Spices like turmeric, ginger, and garlic

You should also make it a point to maintain good oral health. Brush and floss at least twice a day, and visit your dentist every six months or as recommended by your dentist for check-ups and a professional clean. This will stop harmful bacteria in your mouth from working their way to your gut.

Finally, avoid sugary foods. They cause inflammation and boost the growth of yeast, which can throw off your gut balance (Almekinder, n.d.). You should also avoid artificial sweeteners such as saccharine, which harm your gut health. To sweeten food, opt for natural products like stevia.

ENJOY A LITTLE ME-TIME

When you are a parent, it can seem like you are forced to divide yourself into so many roles that you have little time to simply be alone with your thoughts. This can be particularly distressing if you are introverted and are forced to deal with various people, including doctors, therapists, and other parents, during your week. Try to spend a little me-time every day so you can collect your thoughts and enjoy the silence.

KNOW WHEN TO SEEK PROFESSIONAL HELP

In Chapter Five, you read about the importance of seeing a therapist if you need one. Your family may also benefit from psychotherapy if issues such as silence, substance abuse, trauma, anger issues, behavioral problems, depression, and/or anxiety are present. If rough patches last for months and it seems like brighter days are few and far between, it may be time to ask for recommendations for an experienced therapist.

CHAPTER SUMMARY

There will always be something to do, attend to, or fix when it comes to your family, but remember that caring for yourself is a must. If you are feeling anxious or depressed despite taking proactive steps to exercise self-kindness and lower stress, seek professional help. If you have been feeling tired, unmotivated, or run-down lately, ask yourself the following questions:

1. Do I try to focus on the many things I have achieved and celebrate small and larger victories alike?
2. Do I engage in healthy practices such as exercise, journaling, holistic practices, and/or creative pursuits?
3. Do I make time for myself to do the things that give my life meaning and purpose?
4. Do I have people to talk to, and if so, do I feel free to share my thoughts and emotions with them?
5. Do I get a good night's sleep?
6. Am I consuming healthy meals every day and avoiding feel-good foods like sugar, which can harm my gut health?

7. Have I built healthy routines that I am able to stick to?
8. Do I have enough time alone to meditate, read, or put my thoughts in order?

Try to get to the point where the answer to every one of these questions is a resounding "yes!"

Help Me Make Waves!

You know how tough it can be to parent a child with autism... And you also know how rewarding it can be. Now's your chance to help other parents like you navigate these complicated waters.

Just a few sentences on Amazon letting other readers know how this book has helped you could make a world of difference to a family.

WANT TO HELP OTHERS?

Thank you for joining me on my mission to help parents of autistic children all over the world. Alone, I can make a splash... With your help, I can make waves.

Scan this QR code for the review link.

CONCLUSION

Autism is a lifelong developmental disability that can impact your child's communication skills, relationships, and self-regulation skills. When you receive a diagnosis, it can feel overwhelming since, in a matter of days, you will probably have to take in a host of information and make many decisions.

From the outset, let self-kindness and evidence guide you. Be proactive, but give yourself time to read up on everything from the nature of autism to tried-and-tested as well as more novel approaches. Know that you will most likely go through various stages (awareness, acceptance, appreciation, and action) before you feel ready to make important decisions.

A diagnosis does not change who your child is. They are the same fun, loveable, unique, and intelligent person they were before. All it does is give you information about how your child thinks, processes, and experiences the world.

 He is 9. Just got diagnosed. I was fine. He is the same kid he was the day before.

CONCLUSION

TARA LOPES

Knowledge is a priceless asset. It enables you to confidently choose everything from the best professionals for your child to the school that matches their learning style and personality. Knowledge is something you should continually strive for. Stay abreast of new discoveries, treatments, and approaches. Don't fall for miracle cure traps, but do stay open to new and successful evidence-based approaches.

Taking an open, honest stance towards your child's diagnosis can lift a big burden from your shoulders. You may encounter people who are unaware of what autism is, and they may say things that hurt your or your child's feelings. However, it can help to see these challenging situations as opportunities to boost autism awareness. Not everyone will be open and interested in what you are saying, but you may be positively surprised by the many people who are.

There are many myths about autism that you will debunk one by one. Typical falsehoods include the idea that people with autism are not interested in social interaction or that they all have either a savant skill or an intellectual disability. Children with autism can have challenging behaviors. For instance, they can rely on stimming or raise their voice if they feel overwhelmed. However, there are many approaches that can help them gain vital skills in areas like self-calming, reading non-verbal body language, understanding the subtle nuances of language, and similar areas. Be prepared to try out a few therapies. Your medical team, autism resources, and other parents may recommend different approaches. This includes cognitive-behavioral therapy, occupational therapy, and social skills training. Your child is not the only one who may benefit from training. Behavior intervention training for parents can be an invaluable way to manage behavioral problems. Psychotherapy, meanwhile, can help you cope with the stress of adaptation and teach you more fruitful ways to think, feel, and behave.

One thing that will become clear as the months and years go by is that this disorder is not linear. It is a spherical spectrum with great variation from person to person. Thus, some autistic children may benefit from help with language but have a high level of motor skills. Some may easily become overwhelmed by sounds and light, while others may not mind noises and crowds at all. Therefore, you may have to experiment with various types of therapy and activities that benefit your child before you find the combination that will help them thrive.

Maintaining a proactive, positive attitude and a growth mindset is important, but you should also be aware of the challenges you and your family may have to face. Autism can be financially stressful, especially if one person has to quit their job or reduce their hours to care for their child and take them to different appointments throughout the week. Parents may also find that they lack the time they need for self-care.

List the challenges you meet along the way and take a solutions-based approach to each of them. If you find that you are tired, is there any way you can free up some-time for yourself? Accept the support that loved ones wish to give you and give yourself the time you need to keep your physical and mental health in good condition. If you find that there is tension in your family or that relationships are strained, consider family therapy to improve communication and learn the techniques you need to remain united and face the challenges you meet as a team.

If you have other children, explain to them what autism is, teach them how to interact with their autistic sibling, and allow them to share their feelings with you, both positive and negative. Teach them key emotional regulation skills. Ensure that rules are fair and consistent for all your children, and make sure everyone has chores to do.

Some changes you may need to make are practical. For instance, designing an autism-friendly home can help your child feel safe and calm at home. You will also need to invest in safety measures to reduce the risk of accidents and elopement. Cutting-edge technological devices such as GPS tracking devices can be a big help, as can the awareness of your neighbors.

Brush up on the law and research the entitlements that can ensure your child has the appropriate educational plan. Making financial arrangements and ensuring your insurance covers most of your child's medical needs are also important. Research will also enlighten you about any financial help you may be entitled to, including grants, government benefits, government assistance, and similar programs.

One of the biggest decisions you will make involves your child's future. Will they be financially secure when you are no longer around? Seeing a financial advisor and a lawyer specializing in wills and trusts is important. You should appoint a guardian for your child and plan for their future living arrangements.

Once the big decisions are out of the way, you can really concentrate on how to organize your day-to-day life so you can meet your many obligations effectively. From the start, keep an accurate, well-organized record-keeping system, both for online and printed documents. You should also establish a routine using visuals to let your child know all the things that need to be done every day.

Another goal that takes time is figuring out the best ways to deal with inappropriate behavior. It is very important to identify your child's triggers and to give them some control over their daily tasks, so they can grow in confidence. You will most likely find that teaching them self-calming techniques, using positive reinforcement, and ignoring some negative behaviors will take you far.

Observe your child so you understand what they need, and when you communicate with them, use clear language and short sentences to reduce confusion. Your child may struggle when it comes to adjusting to changes. Of course, life sometimes forces us to veer from our routines. When you do, use tools like social stories to prepare them beforehand.

Be on the lookout for signs of bullying; children with autism have a higher likelihood of being victims of this behavior. By acting early, you can prevent the long-term consequences that bullying can have on your child's physical and mental health.

Your everyday or weekly life should include activities that support your child's growth. Exercise, play dates, and hobbies can all fill a child's week with great memories that also hone their skills in key areas. Focus on their strengths and interests, and give them the opportunities and tools they need to let their talents shine. As your child grows older and develops interests, encourage them to volunteer, take up further study, or find employment. Doing so will boost their independence and help expand their social circle.

Finally, make sure to take care of yourself. You are your child's parent, friend, and staunchest advocate. Be kind to yourself, just as you are to the people you love. Acknowledge the many things you have accomplished and reward yourself by taking part in activities you enjoy and spending time with people outside your home. Try to ensure that you fulfill many roles, not just that of a parent. Take up the hobbies you have always loved or learn new ones. Try to ensure you have at least 10 minutes of me-time every day, eat well, exercise daily, embrace holistic stress-busting techniques, and don't neglect the things that give you satisfaction and joy.

If there is one thing most parents have in common, it is the big change most experience from the time their child is first diagnosed to just one or two years later.

 My son was 18 months old when diagnosed. I didn't know anything about autism. I know I felt alone, clueless, not sure what would happen, so many questions and felt shocked also, but years later, I understand it all now. It's funny how things change just like that. You never know.

[NAME WITHHELD]

CONCLUSION

Through trial and error, reading, speaking to others, therapy, and behavioral training, all parents eventually understand that autism is not an impediment to raising a healthy, happy child who can sustain meaningful relationships, make friends, and find passions, interests, and talents.

Autism is not who your child is, so don't let it affect how you see and relate to them. Instead, see your child as the flexible, malleable individual that all human beings are. Focus on maintaining a growth mindset, on seeing failures as opportunities for growth, and on experimenting with evidence-based approaches until you find those that click with your child. Remember that autism is a spectrum disorder. All children have strengths and weaknesses. It is up to you to help your child gain the skills they need to improve their weaknesses and also to provide them with the experience, education, training, and tools they need to shine at the things they are passionate about.

If you found this book helpful and think that it can help others who are coming to terms with an autism diagnosis, please leave a review on Amazon and help reach others who may find value in the insights and advice in this book.

Scan this QR code for the review link.

APPENDIX I

PARENTS REACT TO THE DIAGNOSIS

The following question was asked of parents and grandparents in several autism support groups:

How old was your child when diagnosed and what was your reaction?

Their comments are included with permission and have been copyedited to correct grammar, spelling, and punctuation. Care has been taken to retain the writer's content, voice, and style.

"My daughter is 16 and what a relief! I knew due to my own extensive research but no doctor would officially diagnose until we finally got in to see a psychiatrist. And what an amazing change it made in my daughter. We are finally learning how to live with it, I guess. A lot fewer meltdowns. " – *Amanda Reis*

"23 months. Kind of surprised. I thought she would have to be 6 or 7 for a diagnosis. Didn't know it could be as early as 18 months." — *C.J. Jennings*

"My daughter was diagnosed two months before she turned 2. We somewhat saw it coming because we noticed it and we were the ones who brought it up to her doctor. But mentally, I don't think I was as ready as I thought. Husband, you can say, was prepared completely. I guess as a mom you take it more personally." — *Kati Garcia-Rocha*

"My grandson was 2--he's 6½ now. We've had custody since he was born and are almost done with the adoption process. We are fortunate to have a children's hospital with a special autism clinic. We walked out in shock and disbelief. I could not process what we were just told. And of course, we walked out with paperwork for 9 different doctors and testing, and SSI and medicaid, and OPWDD, and the parents' network and the IEP recs and therapy recs and schools, and it just went on and on—' Oh, and by the way--he's speech-delayed and here's 100 pages of what all these alphabets mean, and you can learn about autism.' I was literally destroyed, and the nightmare didn't calm down until last year, when he started kindergarten and all the Covid drama was over. He's in a great school, rocking first grade." — *Monica Smith*

"24 months. He's my 10th grandchild, and I just want to make sure he has everything he needs to flourish and achieve whatever he desires. I pray all these programs and protocols don't try to change him, and I hope we can all learn to meet him where he is." — *Nancy L. Wallace-Stallard*

"He was 4. We were relieved because we had suspected it for a long time and visited almost a dozen professionals to get to that conclusion." — *Lance Newman*

"My first son was 18, had been fighting [for him] for years, and my second son was 16, only just got his diagnosis two months ago." — *Tania Pierce*

"Just under 5 and I felt relief, after 2½ years fighting for him, being pushed from pillar to post, constantly going round in circles." — *Abi Pride*

"My 2½ yr old is awaiting a diagnosis. However, I've known for sure since he was 1. He's got textbook traits. In hindsight, I could see [traits] much younger, but didn't want to admit it to myself." — *Amber Lynass*

"I knew at age 2, but honestly never got the official diagnosis for him. My daughter was almost 9. I was shocked because I was made to believe I was crazy for thinking she had autism just as well as her older brother. I was relieved that I wasn't as crazy as I was made to feel I was." — *Alissa Dyer*

"1½ and I was expecting it, so I was relieved and optimistic. (Still am)." — *Connie Miniaci*

"4 and I was sad but relieved." — *Clare James*

"Myself and the kids were 42, 10¾, 8, and yet my 20 year old is still waiting. I was chucked to bits for finally being heard and getting the support I needed." — *Heather Rose*

"11 and although I knew she would be diagnosed, I was scared and felt as though I wasn't good enough for her. Then I picked myself up and learned how to be good enough." — *Jessica Blair*

"Having the diagnosis actually helps in the long run. With my daughter, they took her in the room and asked her a bunch of questions and watched her play. Told stories and had her tell them stories. We didn't get the results on the day, but some do." — *Julie Potter*

"I knew from the age of 2, finally diagnosed at age 9, and I cried my eyes out! Someone finally listened to me!" — *Kelz Diane Gregson*

"My son was 3. I knew from 18 months he was possibly autistic, was still a shock when he was actually diagnosed though. It took a while to process, but at the same time, I was relieved and I knew I wasn't crazy." — *Lauren L Loveley*

"My son was about 2yrs old and I wanted to know through evaluation. Yes or no, whatever diagnosis was given, I would work with him from there. I enrolled my son in a birth-to-three program. When he turned 4, teachers worked with him. He received special education and speech. My son has developmental delays as well. Every day is a day of progress. At times, it gets hard for me. I need to learn how to turn my head to the behavior that I don't understand and praise the behavior that I do understand. My son is verbal. He can dress himself and put on his shoes. He may put his shoes on the wrong foot, but he tries. Any help on how to better work with my son to help me not feel like I have failed him would be appreciated. Be blessed everyone." — *Laytricia Wyatt*

"3 and happy knowing, just went into crazy mode educating myself. I have never grieved him." — *Melanie Kate*

"I have 2 on the spectrum. Both were diagnosed around 3. I was in denial with my first. By the time I had my second and noticed the signs, I immediately talked to her doctor to get the process started." — *Mika Madison*

"My son was born at 23 weeks weighing 1 pound, 2 oz. So he's always been delayed. They diagnosed him at around 9 months. He's about to be 5 next week and still has some developmental delays, won't get along with other children, and still only eats orange or tan items. It's still hard taking him out places, but he's alive and healthy so it's still a win for me. He had a 20% chance of survival." — *Paris Yarbrough*

"12 and I felt victory because finally someone actually listened to me. — *Princess Stacy Parker*

"1½. Very upset, because he's my first. I thought it was a bad thing, but as he grew, my knowledge of ASD also grew. We both grew together." — *Taylor Proctor*

"2½, but I'd known it for around 13 months." — Rebecca Forsh

APPENDIX 2

PARENT OPINIONS OF ABA

The following question was asked of parents and grandparents in several autism support groups.

What are your thoughts about ABA?

Their comments are included with permission and have been copyedited to correct grammar, spelling, and punctuation. Care has been taken to retain the writer's content, voice, and style.

"ABA in its initial inception was far different than most ABA practices now. Back then, it was more important to crank out "uniformity at all costs." For my son in his center, ABA focuses on helping the individual navigate the society we have without suppressing the emotions and feelings of the autistic individual. For example, going to the dentist/doctor/barber was a hellacious struggle for us to the point where they were recommending he be drugged to be compliant for an exam. I refused, and through social stories and positive reinforcement, his ABA team showed him that these people mean no harm and want to help, as well as some mindfulness exercises to get him through the appointments. None of this was done to make him blindly compliant. Medical care is important and the sedation process can be traumatizing too, as you'd have to hold them down to get the sedation going." — *Aimee Dunn*

"Every place is different. Please don't take into account others' negative experiences if they did punishing. My daughter is level 3 severe autistic. She goes to ABA every day from 8-3. I would do more if my schedule allowed. But she has flourished there, and she's only been there a month and a half. She makes more eye contact, answers to her own name, and even helps dress herself now. I can't say enough good things about all the therapists that work with her and the director as well. She was uncomfortable for maybe the first few weeks because it was out of routine for her, but now we get to the door and she waits for them to let us in. Every parent has a different experience. So please keep that in mind." — *Ashley Nicole*

"I both work in ABA and my son is in ABA. I can definitely see how it can be harmful if not done properly. It's come a long way from when it first started. One of my kiddos at work I've been on for 7 months and he is doing things people never thought possible. My son has only been in ABA since July and has made MAJOR steps. He's doing things and practicing skills that I could only dream of a few months ago. Do your research into your local facilities. Go on tours. Talk to other parents. It's not for every child with autism. But it can definitely be helpful to a lot of kids." — *Ashley Nicole Powell*

"I work at an ABA center as an RBT and many are arguing that in ABA we do not look for the "why" of the behavior and that we try to stop behaviors in order to make an autistic child act "normal." At the center I work for, we look for the reason the behavior is being presented by the child and teach them how to cope with the problem. We don't punish the children for stimming or simply being autistic. Instead, we teach them how to cope in the real world and help them to recognize what is overwhelming to them. We celebrate their differences and teach them how to use their differences to their own advantage. I mean, we guide our neurotypical kids, and the way we do that is by teaching them how to be productive members of society! So why should it be different for our neurodivergent kiddos?" — *Demi Lynn Bolley*

"Best thing we did for my 4 Y.O! After a few months in ABA he transitioned to their Preschool Therapeutic school. He always has a RBT behind him in school just like the other kids in his class. He is thriving at school and at home. " — *Jennifer Saechao*

"There should never be any punishment for being autistic, ever! Coping mechanisms do not last and aren't always healthy or effective for the autistic generally. If he has maladaptive behavior, specific trauma therapy would probably be more helpful. If he still has frustration and his nervous system is being triggered to fight, he's still in a situation that causes trauma. This is why many autistic adults state ABA contributes towards PTSD markers in early adulthood. Coping mechanisms usually install a trauma response deeper. The problem is the abject discrimination of the mainstream society in the 'real world.' They need adults and parents who advocate for them and seek to create a more conducive environment for the nature of the autistic child, not embedding a trauma response even deeper. It would be more productive for the adult caregivers and so-called helpers to petition for awareness and social change and acceptance of the autistic child than pushing it all on the child." — *Louise Scargill*

"I could put signs all over my yard, go to rallies and post on social media, but that wouldn't change how other kids look at my autistic boys when they are throwing themselves on the floor because they don't want to leave, pushing kids at the water park, running when they're not supposed to, not listening when I yell and have to tackle them, etc. I don't want my kids to suffer more heartache than they have to because they have no idea how to act in society. I want them to grow up to be functional adults who can get a job, be married, have kids, and whether it's autism or some other issue that causes kids to not be able to do those things, I believe parents' role is to guide them in the right direction. There will be much more heartache in the long run if they don't learn these basic skills. I'm sure they would prefer to continue running away from us in front of cars in parking lots, knocking kids over in playgrounds because they don't even notice them, never sit during story time or table time, not sit down at the table while eating, not communicating with us or anybody else, never getting potty trained, brushing their teeth or cutting their hair for the rest of their childhood. But is that what's best for them? Is that what's best for any child? Most children don't want to do those things, but they have to as well. I didn't want to do chores, work on the family farm when I was a kid or take piano lessons, but it wasn't my choice, and I am better off for it. The role of parents is to guide their children to live a healthy life and set them up for the most success possible. Allowing them to do whatever they want is not good parenting. I would like for my 3½ old boys to be able to communicate beyond the level of a 6-month old baby, which is where they're currently at. I would like them to be able to pull their own pants up and down and eventually put their shoes on. These are things ABA is currently helping with, and it's nothing extraordinary. I want them to be able to have a chance one day to be in classes with non-special needs kids. Right now, we are nowhere near that. — *Kay Tee*

"I was dead set against ABA at first but I love my son too much to deny him any chance at a good life. I did the research. I did the searching to find my son the perfect fit and nothing less. My son has made major progress in less than six months since he's been attending. My son is thriving and is celebrated every day for who he truly is, and I wouldn't trade this for the world. It's been life changing and the people at the clinic have become almost like family. He absolutely loves and adores every single person that works at his clinic and loves his friends. They teach him self-love and how to be confident. They teach my son to love and embrace his autism, and they guide him to find healthy and safe ways to deal with overwhelming situations. They also guide him on how to find ways to regulate. They love his flappy hands and his vocal stims. They love every single thing about him, nothing less. And they celebrate every little thing about him, autism and all. Not a single BCBA or RBT at his clinic would want to teach my son that his autism is wrong. His ABA doesn't tell him how to conform to NT expectations. I would never put my son through something like that. His ABA therapy shouldn't even be called ABA because it's mostly learning through play with peers. Where the kids are guiding their therapists through their curriculum and the therapists are just giving them many options and opportunities for growth. But I'm trying to spread awareness that not all ABA is like that anymore. I wouldn't change my son's autism for the world, but yes, I would like to give him the opportunity to learn how to acknowledge his emotions and understand them. He's a child who doesn't know why he gets angry the way he does or why he gets overwhelmed the way he does, and his therapists help him find that understanding while letting HIM guide the proper forms of regulation that he enjoys. They also teach me how to understand him better and how I can help him thrive at home and at school. Not once have they tried to teach us how to stop my son from being autistic. I just sincerely believe that the modern ABA is life changing. And if parents tried it and still don't think it's right for them, then at least they tried it. Also, I'm not invalidating autistic people and their views on ABA because I'm sure they experienced the worst of it in the past years. But completely bashing on it will scare parents away from what ABA is now, and it isn't fair to the children who can really benefit from the new practices and principles. It's very life changing for our kids. Open your mind up to the possibility that there are actually good people in this world who love and care for our children on the spectrum and want to see them succeed. Do your research and visit ABA clinics and sit down with their BCBAs and RBTs. That's why I say do your research and find the right fit because not every ABA therapist is horrible and not every ABA therapist is amazing. Otherwise you're just fear mongering and letting parents unknowingly deny their children services that can change their lives for good." — L. D.

"My daughter is in ABA therapy now and there is no "punishment" whatsoever, only positive reinforcement. They do a full analysis of why and when the "unusual" behaviors occur. This center does not address stimming behaviors unless they are harmful or really affect the learning process. I am describing my daughter's experience only." — *Liudmyla Lang*

"I had an appointment with a behavioral therapist and didn't bring my son. He instantly went into ABA. It was purely horrifying what he was saying he would work on with my son! It's made to train your child to act like an NT; it's torture for autistic people." — *Melanie Kate*

"Our BCBA refuses to stop stimming or correcting the behaviors associated with autism. My child is level 3, non-verbal. Her ABA model is teaching communication. She doesn't force eye contact either. Every therapist is different, and if you're in a private clinic and not a center (yes, there's a difference), you will find a different model of teaching. My son is learning at ABA and is not being forced to stop his stimming. He's 3; he sings, counts, and can name 50 animals and put them in their correct climate. Not to mention the unlimited number of different objects he can name when asked. My son started at a time when he was lost in a world I knew nothing about. He didn't talk, look up, or respond. Now 10 months into ABA, he's doing all these things I only dreamed he could one day do. People need to sit in until they fully understand their therapist and how they teach. I sat in on sessions for 2 months until I was comfortable enough to allow him to be there because I do not agree with suppressing autism. I want him to shine as an autistic and that's exactly what his therapist emphasizes." — *Michelle Green*

"ABA— I would suggest reading up on it. From autistic people themselves, not from the "professionals." The thing is, ABA focuses on making autistic children seem more "normal." By removing the autistic behavior (hand flapping, stimming etc). But they do it by negative reinforcement (punishment). Taking away toys, withholding a promised reward etc., without looking into WHY the child has the behavior. Look at it this way: if I decided I didn't want you to pick your nose, that was an unwanted behavior. By punishing you every time you did it, I would be able to make you stop, but it would not make the itch go away. You would still have the impulse to pick your nose because something was itching. This is the same with ABA. It has results. Yes, it removes autistic behavior, but at what price? It doesn't remove the impulse/trigger for the behavior, so the child just gets frustrated. A lot of parents also notice that after stopping ABA, the behavior reoccurs, simply because the child is no longer afraid of punishment. IF you want to do this ABA therapy, I would recommend that you insist on being present at all times and to pull your child out if they even mention the punishment/withholding rewards. Also, I would insist on a plan for the therapy. What is the goal? Fine if the goal is communication skills or potty training. Not so fine if the goal is to make the child appear neurotypical (desensitivity training). We cannot be "desensitized". Our brains simply don't work that way. We don't have the filter that neurotypical brains have, and you can't "train" something you don't have. There are TONS of different forms of therapy that are both more successful and do not cause PTSD, so why should parents "hunt around" for the few ABA therapists that are "good?" A chance of a "good life?" So you think that the only way an autistic person gets a good life is by blending in with NTs? Sorry for the long rant. It's really something that sets me off, and I hate that such medieval methods are still being used today, because parents don't know what it does to their children." — *Nadja Camilla Aagaard Dueholm*

"My friend's son has transformed incredibly well into a fine young man with ABA therapy. He had so many challenges before the therapy. I have certainly changed my mind after seeing how he is now compared to before. ABA is all dependent on the therapist, just like you can have a good or bad teacher. It's like saying, 'I hate all history teachers because one racist, awful one put me off.' And I have read positive cases of autistic adults who have thrived, so not all autistic adults suffered. My son has learned to speak, put his clothes on and off, eat with cutlery and potty train. Please explain how this is abuse? Speech therapy and OT was a complete waste of time for us compared to ABA but I wouldn't say all OT and SALT are bad, hence I don't think all ABA is bad. A lot of people use indirect ABA and they don't even know it. There is zero evidence that its unhealthy, only hearsay and 99% of people saying it's bad have never tried it, while everyone says positive things have tried it. 99% of autism schools in my area use ABA." — *Sal Adam*

"My son was never punished or had things taken from him as punishment. Do research on your own ABA offices near you and pick one that's a right fit for your family! Trying to help your baby in every way possible is the goal! Not everyone has the same experiences." — *Salycia Cece Barrera*

"Psychologist here, and I am against it. I am an autistic person with autistic children. I see so many NTs defending ABA, and they don't understand. As of yet, I have not met any other autistic adults who will tell you they like ABA in any capacity. I've been put through ABA. The last attempt was less than 10 years ago, while I was a highschooler. I have complex PTSD due to ABA practices. If anyone would actually like to listen to other autistic people's perspectives on the subject and be actually interested in what we have to say and not just what makes your lives easier, I have some great groups of autistic adults who can provide further insight, studies, statistics, and other information related." — *Sari Pevec*

"It's a 'no' from us. I don't agree with punishment for behavior that is caused by illness or condition. It's like punishing a child who has fits due to epilepsy or something in my mind. I don't use fear and control in my parenting either. I choose not to reinforce by punishment of behavior. I wouldn't like it if someone came and took my shit because I behaved in a way that they didn't think was acceptable. I prefer other methods like positive reinforcement for good behavior, reflection and teaching good behavior to replace negative behaviors and alternative things/strategies to use to avoid said behavior being repeated. Behavior and reinforcement have better outcomes and stick with long term reinforcement and reward, that is proven in theory so it blows my mind that they use punishment to teach not to use behavior that allows a neurodivergent child or adult to emotionally regulate. I mean I tap my leg, play with my hair, fiddle with small objects, and pick my face when emotionally dysregulated, stressed or such. I can't explain the response a person would get if they started trying to punish me for them. I'd also question if removing one wouldn't cause it to manifest in a different way or cause escalation in other behaviors such as irritability, anger, and the rest due to lack or regulation. I'd also worry it would be traumatizing. Autistic people are traumatized much easier than typical people and could imagine the kind of stress and toll therapy and repeated negative consequences would have on a person, I would worry it would affect sense of self, confidence, and other core identity things. And lastly, I accept my autistic child for everything he does and the person he is, the same as I accept my typical children. If I was addressed by someone who didn't, they'd be the issue in the equation and they'd be removed, not the child and their behaviors. However, that said, if someone did use it, I wouldn't judge them either. We parent in our own way and take positives with negatives and see the world/kids/issues differently. If you feel that's what's best for your child, I'd still support that regardless too." — *Stacey Keepi*

"I am a 3rd generation autistic with two grown autistic children. As a professional, the new guidelines still leave much to be desired. They reward unnatural behaviors for a neurodiverse individual. They reduce stimming, want eye contact (which can actually be painful for autistic individuals) and "train" children to fall in line. Much better is an occupational therapist who has expertise with neurodivergent children. Punishment for neurotypicals is not the same as punishing neurodivergent individuals. If an autistic child needs a toy red truck to self regulate and the truck is withheld, that is punishment and quite detrimental. Stipulate that you prefer the focus to be on occupational therapy using things your child loves. Eg if they love playing with leaves, then play should center around leaves, not have leaves with-drawn (punishing) until the task is completed. Favorite things must be integrated into the therapy. Stipulate that healthy stims should be encouraged and that eye contact shouldn't be forced. If they are happy to accommodate these needs for your child, then they are responsive and hopefully just using the banner of ABA for funding purposes. If they say it won't work unless they do it the way it's designed, then that is a red flag and you may want to reconsider. Meanwhile, see if there are other funded options in your area so that you have a fallback plan. Remember, you know what your child looks like when they are happy and thriving. You know what happy stims they have and what happy noises they make. Let those guide you." — *Stephanie Astro* (https://www.facebook.com/StephAstroASCSupport)

"My son graduated from ABA and is now in K. He has a classmate that is level 1/2 and can fully respond to you but has times where they can stim greatly or scream suddenly. My son benefited very well, but about 6 months in, he wasn't showing any improvements, just a plateau effect. I still thought it was very helpful. He has learned/improved so much in communication from when he was diagnosed at level 3. To the people that are against it: have they actually tried it and, more impor-tantly, how significant are their child's behaviors? I feel ABA helps the more significant levels, especially ones deemed non-verbal. Some, like mine, level 3 and even level 2, were not connected to the world or showed more disruptive behaviors in the classroom environment. I don't know. I am not against ABA because I felt it helped significantly. My suggestion: just try a few months and see the potential improve-ments:)" — *Travis Bennett*

"My 10 year old is autistic and I'm an RBT and implement ABA for autistic children. Progressive ABA done properly by well trained professionals involves the reinforcement of positive behaviors, correct answers/responses, or approximations of them, etc. We also reinforce the absence of aberrant behaviors when they typically arise, such as hitting, spitting, screaming, and engaging in tantrum behaviors, etc. at inappropriate times. Those behaviors are ignored or the client is redirected or talked to about the importance of doing things such as following directions. So I don't see why people are saying some of the things I'm reading, and why they're so angry. People are literally commenting like 'Grr, I hate ABA! Things like positive reinforcement should be used instead!' Like..dude you're literally describing a major aspect of ABA!" — *Lauren Bouldin*

CONTRIBUTORS

I want to sincerely thank these parents and grandparents for sharing their thoughts, their experiences, and their lives as they stand strong for their children and grandchildren every day. We can all learn from them and be better for it. With warmest regards – L.T.

Sal Adam
Debbie Anderson
Jess Ann
Stephanie Astro
(https://www.facebook.com/StephAstroASCSupport)
Annabett Avery
Salycia Cece Barrera
Travis Bennett
Jessica Blair
Demi Lynn Bolley
L. D.
Nadja Camilla Aagaard Dueholm
Aimee Dunn
Alissa Dyer
Keily J Fairhead

CONTRIBUTORS

Rebecca Forsh
Kati Garcia-Rocha
Michelle Green
Kelz Diane Gregson
Brooke Hanson
Carol Hinch
Clare James
C.J. Jennings
Ryan Jones
Melanie Kate
Stacey Keepin
Suzanne Kohler
Liudmyla Lang
Tara Lopes
Lauren L Loveley
Amber Lynass
Mika Madison
Tyler Martin
Holly Molina
Clare McGovern
Connie Miniaci
Lance Newman
Ashley Nicole
Marcella Noster
Princess Stacy Parker
Sari Pevec
Tania Pierce
Julie Potter
Ashley Nicole Powell
Abi Pride
Taylor Proctor
Julianne Regan
Amanda Reis
Heather Rose
Jennifer Saechao

CONTRIBUTORS

Louise Scargill
Monica Smith
KatiTee
Nancy L. Wallace-Stallard
Stephanie Wood
Laytricia Wyatt
Paris Yarbrough

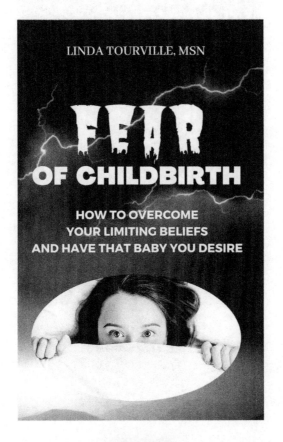

the
PREGNANCY HANDBOOK
for
FIRST-TIME MOMS

A Comprehensive Guide
Covering Weekly
Fetal Development,
Maternal Changes,
Prenatal Tests,
and Making
Informed Decisions

LINDA TOURVILLE, MSN

REFERENCES

ACES. (2021, January 15). *Tips to handle your child's autism diagnosis.*

Ali, D. D. (2015, June 11). *How to handle your child's autism diagnosis.* Parents.

Ali, D. D. (2015, April 8). *A day in the life: Raising a child with autism.* Parents.

Almekinder, E. (n.d.). 6 ways to improve gut health. Blue Zones.

Ambitious about Autism. (n.d.). *Using visual stories.*

Anand, N. (2021, February 20). *Common challenges of parenting an autistic child.* Caliber.

Ashburn, M. (2019, October 24). *Before you start grieving for your autistic child…* Not an Autism Mom.

Askham, A. V. (2020, October 15). *Brain structure changes in autism, explained.* Spectrum News.

Autism Society. (n.d.). *Letter of intent.*

Autism Society. (n.d.). *Safety in the home.*

Autism Speaks. (2016, February 16). *The do's & don'ts after an autism diagnosis.*

Autism Speaks. (n.d.). *100 day kit for young children.*

Autism Speaks. (n.d.). *Autism statistics and facts.*

Autism Speaks. (n.d.). *Parent's guide to autism.*

Autism Speaks. (n.d.). *Reacting to the diagnosis.*

Autism Speaks. (n.d.). *What causes autism?*

Autism Western Australia. (n.d.). *What are the common misconceptions of autism?*

Autistic Self Advocacy Network. (n.d.). *Your vote counts: A self-advocate's guide to voting in the U.S.*

Bears, K., Johnson, C., & Smith, T. Effect of parent training vs parent education on behavioral problems in children with autism spectrum disorder. (2015, April 21). *JAMA, 313* (15), 1524-1533.

Bernick, M. (2021, October 4). *Americans with autism have never had more support—except when it comes to employment.* Politico.

Brady Cobin Law Group, PLLC. (2021, February 26). *Here are some tips for creating an estate plan that benefits a child with special needs.*

Breslow, M. H. (2019, July 1). *Housing for adults with autism: A growing crisis.* Autism Spectrum News.

Bullock, B. G. (2020, October 20). *How mindfulness serves parents of autistic children.* Mindful.

Burton, T. I. (2018, September 10). *"Crossfit is my church": How fitness classes provide the meaning that religion once did.* Vox.

Carlisle, G. K., Johnson, R. A., Wang, Z., Brosi, T. C., Rife, E. M., & Hutchison, A. (2020, March 4). Exploring Human–Companion Animal Interaction in Families of Children with Autism.

REFERENCES

Carmen B. Pingree Autism Center of Learning. (n.d.). *6 best autism apps for skill development and confidence in 2021.*

Carmen B. Pingree Autism Center of Learning. (n.d.). *Tips for explaining autism to family, friends, and kids.*

Centers for Disease Control and Prevention. (n.d.). *What is Autism Spectrum Disorder?*

Chakraborty, N. (2018, December 5). *How to ensure a special child is cared for life.* Live Mint.

Children and Family Mental Health. (2009, August 30). *Family therapy for autism: A tool for generating "positive cycles".*

Columbia University Irving Medical Center. (2018, October 22). *In kids with autism, short questionnaire may detect GI disorders.*

Delisle, R. (2021, August 26). *How to tell your child they have autism.* Today's Parent.

DiProperzio, L. (2021, April 8). *How to avoid comparing your child with special needs to other children.* NY Metro Parents.

Dower, E. (2013, November 4). *Being an advocate for your autistic child.* How to Learn.

Drexel University. (2015.). *Key findings from the National Autism Indicators Report: Transition into young adulthood.*

Ehmke, R. (n.d.). *Sharing an autism diagnosis with family and friends.* Child Mind Institute.

Elemy. (2021, December 14). *Expert-recommended strategies for teaching autistic students.*

Elemy. (2021, December 23). *The average annual costs of autism nationwide.*

Elemy. (2021, December 29). *The best autism support groups for parents (state by state).*

Faherty, C. (2014). *Autism: What does it mean to me? A workbook explaining self awareness and life lessons to the child or youth with high functioning autism or aspergers.* Future Horizons.

Fincher, D. R. (2020, March 19). *Autism is a spectrum disorder – Not a linear disorder.* Medium.

Green, S. F. (n.d.). *Is there really a single spectrum for autism?* Psycom.

Head to Health. (n.d.). *Purposeful activity – hobbies.*

Health Talk. (n.d.). *Parents of children on the Autism Spectrum.*

Healthline. (n.d.). *Everything you need to know about autism spectrum disorder (ASD).*

Heasley, S. (2013, September 3). *Few young adults with autism living independently.* Disability Scoop.

Help Guide. (n.d.). *Helping your child with autism thrive.*

Hendren, R. L. (2014, September 19). *New and emerging biomedical treatments for autism.* Psychiatry Advisor.

Honeybourne, V. (2021, June 25). *How to combat negative thoughts and find happiness with ASD.* Autism Parenting.

Hviid, A., Vinsløv Hansen, J., Frisch, M., & Melbye, M. (2019, April 16). Measles, mumps, rubella vaccination and autism. *Annals of Internal Medicine, 170,* 513-520.

IFL Science. (n.d.). *What is the world's most relaxing color? A new survey just found out.*

Interactive Autism Network. (2016, December 9). *The role of neurologists in treating children with autism.*

Interagency Autism Coordinating Committee. (n.d.). *Housing.*

REFERENCES

Kelly's Thoughts on Things. (n.d.). *How a parent of autistic children can make them feel included.*

Koenig, R., & Coffee, L. T. (2017, April 14). *Having a child with autism: 21 things I wish I'd known.* Today.

McIlwee, C. (n.d.). *First steps after receiving an autism diagnosis.* JCFS Chicago.

Meduri, A. M. (n.d.). *Autism special needs checklist: Big kids (aged 6-12).* Kids Health.

Mehta, R. (2021, April 23). *How to plan your finances for a special needs child.* Economic Times.

Meredith, G. R., Rakow, D. A., Eldermire, E. R. B., Madsen, C. G., Shelley, S. P., & Sachs, N. A. (2020, January 14). Minimum time dose in nature to positively impact the mental health of college-aged students, and how to measure it: A scoping review. *Frontiers in Psychology, 10.* [18]

Morin, A. (2021, June 23). *Discipline strategies for children with autism.* Verywell Family.

National Autistic Society. (n.d.). *Dealing with bullying – a guide for parents and carers.*

National Autistic Society. (n.d.). *Stimming.*

Nik Adib, N. A., Ibrahim, M. I., Ab Rahman, A., Bakar, R. S., Yahaya, N. A., Hussin, S., & Wan Mansor, W. N. A. (2019, April 25). Perceived stress among caregivers of children with Autism Spectrum Disorder: A state-wide study. *International Journal of Environmental Research and Public Health, 16*(8), 1468.

One Central Health. (2020, October 30). *10 myths about autism spectrum disorder.*

Operation Autism. (n.d.). *Creating a record system.*

Organization for Autism Research. (n.d.). *Sibling support.*

Otsimo. (2018, September 26). *Social skills training for children with autism.*

Otsimo. (2018, November 24.). *Autism 101: What everyone should know about it.*

Pacer. (n.d.). *How "fidget toys" are helping kids with ADHD.*

Penn State Extension. (n.d.). *Acknowledging children's efforts.*

Platt, R. (2022, January 4). *FAQs about guardianship.* Autism Parenting Magazine.

Powell, F., Kerr, E., & Wood, S. (2021, September 13). *See the average college tuition in 2021-2022.* US News.

Prasad, T. (2017, May 18). *8 mistakes I made as a mom of an autistic child.* The Mighty.

Price, J. (2021, December 1). *How parents can build a support system for adult children with disabilities.* AARP.

Raising Children. (n.d.). *Challenging behaviour: Autistic children and teenagers.*

Raising Children. (n.d.). *Learning and development in autistic children and teenagers.*

Raising Children. (n.d.). *Siblings of autistic children: experiences, relationships and support.*

Ray, M. (2021, August 20). *On beliefs vs. evidence.* Barbell Medicine.

Rudy, L. J. (2021, February 15). *How parenting a child with autism can strain a marriage.* Verywell Health.

Rudy, L. J. (2021, February 7). *Assistive technology for autism.* Verywell Health.

Rudy, L. J. (2021, January 15). *6 important things to know about autism.* Verywell Health.

Rudy, L. J. (2021, November 7). *Coping with grief after an autism diagnosis.* Verywell Health.

Rudy, L. J. (2022, January 21). *Sending an autistic child to public school.* Verywell Health.

REFERENCES

Rusoff, J. W. (2020, March 3). *Advisor with autism helps autistic clients navigate a 'whole other world'*. ThinkAdvisor.

Sample, I. (2021, September 20). *Autism therapy aimed at infants may reduce likelihood of later diagnosis*. The Guardian.

Schmidt, J. (n.d.). *Understanding the differences between an IEP and a 504 plan*. N2Y.

School Psychologist Files. (n.d.). *Which is better, a 504 plan or an IEP?*

Schroder, H. S., Moran, T. P., & Moser, J. S. The effect of expressive writing on the error-related negativity among individuals with chronic worry. (2017, September 8). *Psychophysiology, 55*(2).

Science Daily. (2007, May 16). *Treating oneself kindly when things go badly could be a key to weathering life's challenges, researchers say*.

Science Daily. (2009, March 19). *Key to happiness is gratitude, and men may be locked out*.

Sleep Foundation. (2021, June 24). *How to determine poor sleep quality*.

Support quotes. (n.d.). BrainyQuote.

Sweet, J. (2021, April 5). *How Are Most Kids With Autism Doing? Really Well, Research Confirms*. Verywell Mind.

Szatmari, P., Tombeau Cost, K., Duku, E., Bennett, T., Elsabbagh, M., Georgiades, S., Kerns, C. M., Mirenda, P., Smith, I. M., Ungar, W. J., Vallancourt, T., Waddell, C., Zaidman-Zait, A., & Zwaigenbaum, L. (2021, March 29). Association of child and family attributes with outcomes in children with autism. *JAMA Network Open, 4*(3).

Tanasugarn, A. (n.d.). *Why saying "No" doesn't work*. The Autism Analyst.

The Art of Autism. (2019, March 5). *Understanding the spectrum – A comic strip explanation*.

The Best Schools. (2022, January 6). *Schools for autistic children*.

Tsang, T. (2018, April 2). *MythBusters: Autism is social aversion*. Psychology in Action.

Tsetsos, K., Chater, N., & Usher, M. (2009, June 12). Salience driven value integration explains decision biases and preference reversal. *PNAS, 109* (24), 9659-9664.

University of Rochester Medical Center. (n.d.). *Interacting with a child who has autism spectrum disorder*.

University of Victoria. (n.d.). *How arts benefits us all, as humans*.

U.S. Department of Labor. (n.d.). *Family and Medical Leave (FMLA)*.

Valles-Colomer, M., Falony, G., Darzi, Y., Tigchelaar, E. F., Wang, J., Tito, R. T., Schiweck, C., Kurilshikov, A., Joossens, M., Wijmenga, C., Claes, S., Van Oudenhove, L., Zhernakova, A., Vieira-Silva, S., & Raes, J. (2019, February 4). The neuroactive potential of the human gut microbiota in quality of life and depression. *Nature Microbiology, 4*, 623-632.

Van Keuren, M. (2021, October 27). *Guide to life insurance for parents of children with disabilities*. Bankrate.

Vermeulen, P. (2005). *I am special: a workbook to help children, teens and adults with autism spectrum disorders to understand their diagnosis, gain confidence and thrive*. Jessica Kingsley Publishers.

Wang, K. (n.d.). *17 features for a sensory-friendly, therapeutic kitchen*. Friendship Circle.

Wang, K. (n.d.). *Autistic home decorating: Make your home autism friendly*. Friendship Circle.

REFERENCES

Ward-Sinclair, J. (2017, December 16). *Why we shouldn't be afraid to ask for help: Autism support.* Autistic & Apologetic.

We Rock the Spectrum Kid's Gym. (2020, June 17). *25 words to know when discussing autism.*

Wheeler, M. (n.d.). *Getting started: Introducing your child to his or her diagnosis of autism.* Indiana University Bloomington.

Printed in Great Britain
by Amazon

30572627R00089